TYLER MITCHELL &

GDAL DEVELOPERS

GEOSPATIAL POWER TOOLS

GDAL RASTER & VECTOR COMMANDS

Credits & Copyright

GEOSPATIAL POWER TOOLS
GDAL RASTER & VECTOR COMMANDS
by Tyler Mitchell & GDAL Developers

Published by Locate Press
ISBN: 978-0989421713

Direct permission requests to gsherman@locatepress.com or mail:
Locate Press, PO Box 671897, Chugiak, AK 99567-1897

Editor
   Gary Sherman
Cover Design
   Julie Springer
Interior Design
   Based on Tufte-LaTeXdocument class
Book Website
   http://locatepress.com/gpt
Open Source Content
   http://gdal.org

available for download. The following copyright statements delineate the differences.

Layout, Design and New Material

Open Source Content

Contents

Forward

THE OPEN SOURCE GEOSPATIAL SPHERE WOULD LOOK dramatically different without the comprehensive toolset known as the Geospatial Data Abstraction Library, or in short form, GDAL. The creator, Frank Warmerdam, and additional contributors who are now involved, have made it possible for developers to reuse instead of reinvent. From the humble beginnings of supporting TIFF and Shapefile data access, the library now supports some of the new and leading edge formats such as KML and LIDAR. GDAL sits as a quiet, happy, layer between a wide range of applications in the open source and proprietary worlds. If you are curious, do a scan of your computer for the `gdal.dll` or `libgdal.so` files and you may find other applications already depending on GDAL for reading data.

Where would we be without GDAL? Many developers of different applications, web mapping platforms, scripts and more would have created their own data access drivers. Likewise, many of the existing higher level applications would not have developed so quickly to their current state, having been distracted (or outright discouraged) by the chore of writing their own drivers. And, of course, if we didn't have GDAL, you wouldn't have this book in your hands to enjoy!

The GDAL reference manual has existed for a while, in the form of documents on the project website. For the first time, this compilation has been developed to fit into a convenient book format and size. Improvements in the content, accessibility, and readability have been considered for both hardcopy and electronic readers. All the commands from the reference manual are available between these covers.

In addition to the stock reference manual, a full third of the book contains new material. I have assembled a variety of Common Task Workflows & Examples—application specific examples. Professionals handling geospatial data will appreciate the range of topics covered, from how to convert an image to retrieving data from a WMS—all using GDAL commands.

The hope of making this book available is to support those who are working, in the trenches, with geospatial data. Having a command line reference for this famous set of tools will not only give you all the information you need but will also give you that tactile link to years of work that have went into the project.

It is my pleasure to work with Locate Press to bring this book into print as well as e-book formats so that even more people might enjoy the benefits of the GDAL and OGR utilities. I hope you enjoy the book!

Part I

Getting Started

Table of Contents

1

Book Layout

This book is laid out to help you find the information you need as quickly as possible. It is broken into several major parts, each of which have several chapters by topic or command:

I. **Getting Started**: GDAL introduction and sample data setup

II. **Common Task Workflows & Examples**

III. **GDAL Raster Utilities**: Syntax of all commands

IV. **OGR Vector Utilities**: Syntax of all commands

V. **PROJ.4 Projection Utilities**

VI. **OGR SQL**

VII. **CSV File & VRT XML Formats**

VIII. **Appendix 1 - Projection Library Options**

IX. **Appendix 2 - Data Format Listings**

2

Introduction

The Geospatial Data Abstraction Library (GDAL), including its sub-project OGR, is the preeminent open source data access library. It is used behind most of the open source geospatial applications and also sits behind many of the leading proprietary GIS applications on the market today.

This book introduces you to the various GDAL tools, but if you are interested in the libraries behind the tools check out OpenHUB.net, which gives insight into development activity[1] and more. Figure 2.1, on page 12 shows some of the general statistics of the project. For more details see `https://openhub.net/p/gdal` or browse the GDAL source code on GitHub: `https://github.com/osgeo/gdal`.

Along with the programming libraries come several powerful command line utilities—intended to be run by being typed into a terminal or command prompt window. Among these utilities are tools for examining, converting, transforming, building and analysing data. This book is a collection of the GDAL documentation focused on these utilities. The book also includes substantial new content designed to help guide your use of these utilities in solving your current problems.

[1] GDAL is in active development with over 50 contributors. The top 10 contributors in the last 12 months, as reported on OpenHUB.net, are:

- Even Rouault
- Martin Landa
- Dmitry Baryshnikov
- Kurt Schwehr
- Wolf Bergenheim
- Frank Warmerdam
- Tamas Szekeres
- Kyle Shannon
- Pirmin Kalberer
- Ari Jolma

It is designed to be a reference for quickly finding the right syntax and example usage. In digital versions of the book,[2] you can select a command name in the Table of Contents and it will take you immediately to information on that command.

For GDAL raster utilities see Part III: GDAL Raster Utilities and for OGR vector tools see Part IV: OGR Vector Utilities. Following these sections you'll find material about projection utilities and Appendices covering additional options and supported data formats.

Versions

The syntax and command list in the book reflect GDAL version 1.9 or newer. It is possible that some commands or command options may not be available in earlier versions. Where known, those options that are new to 1.9+ are identified.

Installing

This book does not go into detail about installing GDAL/OGR, however there are several easy ways to do so. Naturally, being an open source project, the source code is available for you to download and compile. The GDAL website contains complete information on building GDAL/OGR.[3]

Linux

On Linux operating systems, most package managers will have a package called GDAL and for developers: GDAL-DEVEL (Fedora), GDAL-BIN (Debian), GDAL-DEV, LIBGDAL-DEV or similar. These packages always include the required support for OGR as well.

Mac OS X

A GDAL package is available via Macports and Homebrew:

```
$ sudo port install gdal
$ brew install gdal
```

Kyngchaos.com is a robust and popular source for frameworks and applications ready for OS X. Grab the *GDAL COMPLETE* package to get started quickly.[4] If you want to build it yourself, see the Kyngchaos build instructions.[5]

[4] http://loc8.cc/kyng1
[5] http://loc8.cc/kyng2

Windows

OSGeo for Windows (OSGeo4W) and MapServer for Windows (MS4W) are two easy to install environments for Windows systems. MS4W is focused on MapServer, the web mapping server application, which relies heavily on GDAL.

GDAL libraries and utilities are included in the MS4W package, which is packaged as a simple zip file that you unzip to your hard drive. No installation is required.[6]

[6] http://maptools.org/ms4w

OSGeo4W allows you to install over 150 different open source geospatial software packages, including GDAL.[7]

[7] http://osgeo4w.osgeo.org

Formats

One the greatest strengths of GDAL/OGR is its broad support for a variety of data formats. A comprehensive list of supported formats is included in the closing part of this book. More information, for both raster[8] and vector[9] formats, is also available on the GDAL website. New and improved formats are added regularly.

Refer to the online links for the most up-to-date listings of the formats that are currently supported.

[8] http://gdal.org/formats_list.html
[9] http://gdal.org/ogr/ogr_formats.html

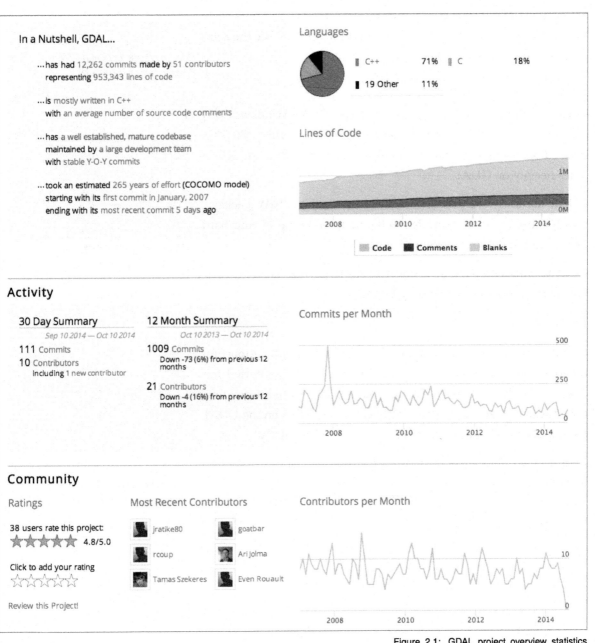

In a Nutshell, GDAL...

...has had 12,262 commits made by 51 contributors representing 953,343 lines of code

...is mostly written in C++ with an average number of source code comments

...has a well established, mature codebase maintained by a large development team with stable Y-O-Y commits

...took an estimated 265 years of effort (COCOMO model) starting with its first commit in January, 2007 ending with its most recent commit 5 days ago

Languages

C++   71%   C   18%
19 Other   11%

Lines of Code

1M
0M
2008   2010   2012   2014
Code   Comments   Blanks

Activity

30 Day Summary
Sep 10 2014 — Oct 10 2014

111 Commits
10 Contributors
Including 1 new contributor

12 Month Summary
Oct 10 2013 — Oct 10 2014

1009 Commits
Down -73 (6%) from previous 12 months

21 Contributors
Down -4 (16%) from previous 12 months

Commits per Month

500
250
0
2008   2010   2012   2014

Community

Ratings

38 users rate this project:
★★★★★ 4.8/5.0

Click to add your rating
☆☆☆☆☆

Review this Project!

Most Recent Contributors

jratike80   goatbar
rcoup   Ari Jolma
Tamas Szekeres   Even Rouault

Contributors per Month

10
0
2008   2010   2012   2014

Figure 2.1: GDAL project overview statistics from https://www.openhub.net/p/gdal

3

Sample Data

There are four sets of data you will need to download to follow the examples in this book. These include both vector and raster datasets suitable for use with the GDAL and OGR tools.

Natural Earth Data

One of the nicest sets of freely available global vector and raster data is from the Natural Earth Data website.[10]

[10] http://loc8.cc/ne

Figure 3.1, on the next page shows the Natural Earth download page and the available data sets. Downloading the *quick start kit*[11] provides a good sampling of the data.

[11] http://loc8.cc/ne_download

Unzipping the download file yields the following directory structure:

```
Natural_Earth_quick_start/
* 10m_cultural
* 10m_physical
* 110m_cultural
* 110m_physical
* 50m_raster
```

Each folder name indicates the intended mapping scale of the data within. For example, 10m means 1:10 million scale. The vec-

Figure 3.1: Natural Earth Data download website

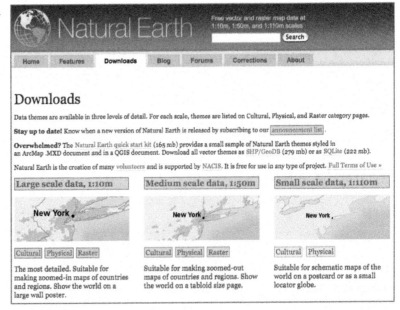

tor datasets are broken into two categories: physical and cultural. There is a raster included as well.

Rename the top/parent folder to ne so it's easier to reference in the examples that follow.

The Natural Earth files provide a core set of example types and formats, however some additional data will also be useful in the more analytical examples we have later on.

GeoNames

GeoNames is a very comprehensive, globally available, *geographic names* dataset. Simply put, this includes as many population centres, lakes, etc. as possible. These are provided in a text format delimited by tabs.

It's not the easiest dataset to work with, that's why we include it!

Download the dataset from geonames.org.[12]

From the website, choose **Free Gazetteer Data**, which links to a download page with `.zip` files for a particular country code (e.g. `CA.zip` for Canada) or `allCountries.zip` to grab everything they've got.

See the bottom of the download page (or the `readme.txt` file included in the zip files) for more details about the structure of the data, field names, etc. Basically it includes an ID number, text describing each name, and a latitude and longitude, along with a few other fields.

For our tests we'll use the `CA.zip` dataset[13].

[13] CA.zip http://loc8.cc/gn_ca

Unzipping it creates a `CA` folder with a `CA.txt` and `readme.txt` file. If you preview the first few lines you will find they look like:

```
5881639 100 Mile House  100 Mile House  51.64982  -121.28594 P PPL  CA  02 ..
5881640 101 Mile Lake   101 Mile Lake   51.66652  -121.30264 H LK   CA  02 ..
5881641 101 Ponds       101 Ponds       47.811    -53.97733  H PNDS CA  05 ..
5881642 103 Mile Lake   103 Mile Lake   51.68312  -121.30265 H LK   CA  02 ..
5881643 105 Mile House  105 Mile House  51.69982  -121.31935 P PPLL CA  02 ..
```

SPOT Satellite Imagery

For more advanced satellite imagery product examples, we use data from SPOT satellites that is freely available from the GeoBase Canada site.[14]

[14] GeoBase: http://loc8.cc/gb

Rather than use only preprocessed data, instead we will use the **Raw Imagery: GeoBase Raw Imagery 2005-2010** datasets. We've selected one scene of data that covers an area near Toronto, Ontario.

Here is how the data are described:

Images of Raw Imagery GeoBase 2005-2010 product are raster digital data coming from SPOT4 and SPOT5 satellites that contain a panchromatic band with 10 meter pixels and a multispectral band with 20 meter pixels.

The example data consists of two `.zip` files and can be downloaded from the FTP site.[15] The files are approximately 30MB each.

[15] SPOT imagery:
http://loc8.cc/spot_dload

Unzipping them, you'll find they include a bunch of ancillary files, including metadata HTML files. The main files we are interested in are the IMAGERY.TIF files. Rename the ...A folder to pan and the folder ending in ...J to multi. This will allow us to easily reference them later on.

We will also be using the primary vol_list.pdf pages from the original imagery capture source to georeference the image in later examples, so keep this data around as well.

Elevation Data

Digital elevation model inputs require a special type of source data. In this case we use data from the Shuttle Radar Topographic Mission (SRTM) for a broad, small scale dataset. You can easily download data for the whole planet, at a reduced resolution. For our purposes, we will use a piece that overlaps the above SPOT imagery location, at a resolution of 90m.

To access the data, visit the CGIAR Consortium for Spatial Information website.[16]

[16] CGIAR CSI: http://loc8.cc/cgi-srtm

After doing a search and selecting the area of interest, we are able to download the source file directly from an FTP site.[17]

[17] SRTM data: http://loc8.cc/srtm_dload

The resulting unzipped files include a GeoTIFF image, a georeferenced *world file* (.tfw) and a *header file* describing the format of the TIFF data that's enclosed. We will mainly be dealing with the srtm_20_04.tif file.

Part II

Common Task Workflows
& Examples

Table of Contents

Common Tasks

This part of the book is specifically designed to help you get up and running with the **Geospatial Power Tools** that are part of the GDAL/OGR toolkit.

There are common tasks that every data manager, analyst, and digital mapmaker has had to deal with and you'll learn most of them; right here, right now!

In the first part of the book we pointed to some sample data that can be used to follow along precisely with the examples illustrated in this part. The latter parts of the book (GDAL and OGR utility syntax parts) do not always follow the same examples or datasets, so if you want some consistent examples, follow along in this part.

The remainder of this chapter presents various examples from the GDAL/OGR command line utilities. They are organised by the general types of commands and give particular focus on their available options.

Each example that follows uses the datasets downloaded in the previous section. In some cases they may be converted/transformed and then used again later. If the original filename, used earlier, is not referenced in further examples then we will provide a link back to the process where the new file was created. If you are reading this as an ebook, simply do a text search for the new filename.

Let's get started...

1

Report Raster Information - gdalinfo

Contents

The two main applications for reporting information about your geographic datasets are: gdalinfo for rasters, and ogrinfo for vector data. This chapter reviews various ways of using the gdalinfo command and its options.

The SRTM data sample described in Chapter 3, Sample Data, on page 13 is used for these examples and an overview is shown in Figure 1.1, on the next page.

List Supported Raster Formats

Run the gdalinfo command with the --formats option to see a list of the raster data formats your version of GDAL/OGR sup-

Figure 1.1: Shaded elevation of the SRTM input data

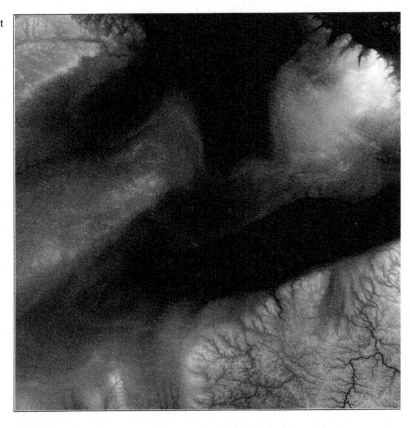

ports. The result also shows whether the format can be used for read and/or write[18]:

[18] 'ro' is read-only driver; 'rw' is read or write; 'rw+' is read, write and update. A 'v' is appended for formats supporting virtual IO.

```
gdalinfo --formats

Supported Formats:
  VRT (rw+v): Virtual Raster
  GTiff (rw+v): GeoTIFF
  NITF (rw+v): National Imagery Transmission Format
  RPFTOC (rov): Raster Product Format TOC format
  HFA (rw+v): Erdas Imagine Images (.img)
  SAR_CEOS (rov): CEOS SAR Image

  ...
```

List raster/image file details

The most basic use of the command requires an input raster file name and lists basic details about the file, in this case an SRTM GeoTIFF format data file:

```
gdalinfo srtm_20_04.tif

Driver: GTiff/GeoTIFF
Files: srtm_20_04.tif
       srtm_20_04.tfw
Size is 6001, 6001
Coordinate System is:
GEOGCS["WGS 84",
    DATUM["WGS_1984",
        SPHEROID["WGS 84",6378137,298.257223563,
            AUTHORITY["EPSG","7030"]],
        AUTHORITY["EPSG","6326"]],
    PRIMEM["Greenwich",0],
    UNIT["degree",0.0174532925199433],
    AUTHORITY["EPSG","4326"]]
Origin = (-85.000416545604821,45.000416884586059)
Pixel Size = (0.000833333333333,-0.000833333333333)
Metadata:
  AREA_OR_POINT=Area
Image Structure Metadata:
  INTERLEAVE=BAND
Corner Coordinates:
Upper Left  ( -85.0004165,  45.0004169) ( 85d 0' 1.50"W, 45d 0' 1.50"N)
Lower Left  ( -85.0004165,  39.9995836) ( 85d 0' 1.50"W, 39d59'58.50"N)
Upper Right ( -79.9995832,  45.0004169) ( 79d59'58.50"W, 45d 0' 1.50"N)
Lower Right ( -79.9995832,  39.9995836) ( 79d59'58.50"W, 39d59'58.50"N)
Center      ( -82.4999999,  42.5000002) ( 82d30' 0.00"W, 42d30' 0.00"N)
Band 1 Block=6001x1 Type=Int16, ColorInterp=Gray
  NoData Value=-32768
```

Compute Min/Max Band Values

Compute the **min/max** values for each band (there is only one band in this example) by adding the -mm option:

```
gdalinfo -mm srtm_20_04.tif
```

```
...
    Min=155.000 Max=537.000
...
```

Compute Band Value Statistics

Compute all available **stats** for each band, by adding the -stats option. This reports the min, max, mean and standard deviation values:

```
gdalinfo -stats srtm_20_04.tif
```

```
...
Band 1 Block=6001x1 Type=Int16, ColorInterp=Gray
 Min=155.000 Max=537.000
 Minimum=155.000, Maximum=537.000, Mean=256.800, StdDev=75.254
 NoData Value=-32768
 Metadata:
   STATISTICS_MAXIMUM=537
   STATISTICS_MEAN=256.80033669602
   STATISTICS_MINIMUM=155
   STATISTICS_STDDEV=75.254180775369
```

Compute Histogram for Bands

Compute the **histogram** for each band, by adding the -hist option to the command:

```
gdalinfo -hist srtm_20_04.tif
```

```
...
Band 1 Block=6001x1 Type=Int16, ColorInterp=Gray
 256 buckets from 154.254 to 537.746:
 466 100 58 112 49 133 ... 609 222 280 265
```

```
NoData Value=-32768
. . .
```

This calculation does a couple things at the same time. First it finds the min and max value (154/537) and then subdivides that range into 256 *buckets* or slices of ranges. Each number reported in the output represents one of those buckets.

Then, the amount of times a pixel value falls into each bucket is counted and reported back, a single number for each bucket: (466, 100, 58, ... 280, 265).

Portions of this histogram are rendered in the graph shown in Figure 1.2. Each vertical bar represents a bucket.

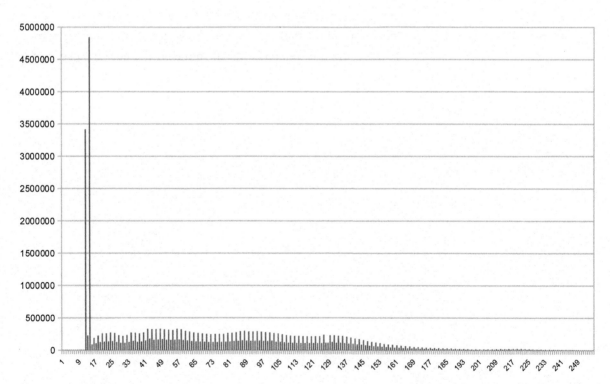

Figure 1.2: Histogram with 256 buckets and pixel counts

Compute Checksum for Bands

Compute a **checksum** value for each band. This value represents a unique, short number value for each band. If any values in the band are changed, the checksum will be different. This provides an easy method for checking if the image has been modified, but without having to open the file programmatically:

```
gdalinfo -checksum srtm_20_04.tif


...

Band 1 Block=6001x1 Type=Int16, ColorInterp=Gray
  Checksum=39711
  NoData Value=-32768
```

Other Options and Flags

The remaining flags and options for gdalinfo just limit some of the information that is output. Read more about those options in the command reference itself, found in the gdalinfo section on page 115.

2

Web Services - Retrieving Rasters (WMS)

Most of these features require a fairly recent version of GDAL [**v1.9+**].

GDAL utilities are able to interact with online web mapping servers that publish raster data using the WMS protocol.[19] There are various permutations and options; these examples are meant to only get you started. See the online documentation for the GDAL WMS driver for more details.[20]

The example service is provided by the Canadian GeoBase.ca group. For more details about their many excellent free products and services, see the website.[21]

[19] OGC WMS specification: http://loc8.cc/wms

[20] GDAL WMS: http://loc8.cc/gdal_wms

[21] GeoBase: http://geobase.ca

Retrieve Layer List of a WMS

There are two components in a WMS request to consider in the following example:

```
gdalinfo WMS:http://ows.geobase.ca/wms/geobase_en

Driver: WMS/OGC Web Map Service
Files: none associated
Size is 512, 512
```

```
Coordinate System is `'
Subdatasets:
  SUBDATASET_1_NAME=WMS:http://ows.geobase.ca/wms/geobase...
  SUBDATASET_1_DESC=Data Collections from GeoBase
  SUBDATASET_2_NAME=WMS:http://ows.geobase.ca/wms/geobase...
  SUBDATASET_2_DESC=Canadian Digital Elevation Data, 1:250,000
  SUBDATASET_3_NAME=WMS:http://ows.geobase.ca/wms/geobase...
    &VERSION=1.1.1&REQUEST=GetMap
    &LAYERS=elevation:cded250k:overview5
    &SRS=EPSG:4269&BBOX=-180,-90,180,90
  SUBDATASET_3_DESC=CDED 1:250,000 level 5 overview
  SUBDATASET_4 ...
```

First, notice that we use the prefix WMS:, telling GDAL which driver to use to open the dataset, and secondly, a URL that points to a WMS resource.[22]

A listing of the *subdatasets* available through the WMS is returned.

For anything but the simplest URL, be sure to surround it with quotation marks. This becomes especially important when adding parameters to the URL as the & symbol has other uses on the command line.

Retrieve Layer Specific Information from a WMS

Naturally you will want more details about a specific layer on the server. Layers can be retrieved using their subdataset numbers. So in the case of the above example, to access SUBDATASET_3, use the -sd n option where n is 3:

```
gdalinfo WMS:http://ows.geobase.ca/wms/geobase_en -sd 3


Driver: WMS/OGC Web Map Service
Files: none associated
Size is 1073741824, 536870912
Coordinate System is:
GEOGCS["NAD83",
    DATUM["North_American_Datum_1983",
```

[22] Instead of a URL, an XML description file can be used. See the GDAL WMS documentation for details.

```
        SPHEROID["GRS 1980",6378137,298.257222101,
            AUTHORITY["EPSG","7019"]],
        TOWGS84[0,0,0,0,0,0,0],
        AUTHORITY["EPSG","6269"]],
    PRIMEM["Greenwich",0,
        AUTHORITY["EPSG","8901"]],
    UNIT["degree",0.0174532925199433,
        AUTHORITY["EPSG","9122"]],
    AUTHORITY["EPSG","4269"]]
Origin = (-180.000000000000000,90.000000000000000)
Pixel Size = (0.000000335276127,-0.000000335276127)
Image Structure Metadata:
  INTERLEAVE=PIXEL
Corner Coordinates:
Upper Left  (-180.0000000,  90.0000000)
Lower Left  (-180.0000000, -90.0000000)
Upper Right ( 180.0000000,  90.0000000)
Lower Right ( 180.0000000, -90.0000000)
Center      (   0.0000000,   0.0000000)
Band 1 Block=1024x1024 Type=Byte, ColorInterp=Red
  Overviews: 536870912x268435456, 268435456x134217728, ...
Band 2 Block=1024x1024 Type=Byte, ColorInterp=Green
  Overviews: 536870912x268435456, 268435456x134217728, ...
Band 3 Block=1024x1024 Type=Byte, ColorInterp=Blue
  Overviews: 536870912x268435456, 268435456x134217728, ...
```

Save a WMS Request as a new Image File

If you enjoy rolling your own URL strings, you can download WMS data directly to disk many different ways. Probably the simplest, aside from using an interactive GUI-based desktop app, is to use gdal_translate after running the first example above to determine the specific layer name you're interested in.

For example, the SUBDATASET_2 layer is one that, after testing in a desktop app, has some nicely shaded elevation maps. Here the layer definition is broken across several lines for clarity:

```
SUBDATASET_2_NAME=
```

```
WMS:http://ows.geobase.ca/wms/geobase_en?SERVICE=WMS
     &VERSION=1.1.1&REQUEST=GetMap&LAYERS=elevation:cded250k
     &SRS=EPSG:4269&BBOX=-180,-90,180,90
SUBDATASET_2_DESC=Canadian Digital Elevation Data, 1:250,000
```

In order to retrieve an image, you'll need at least the correct layer names to include in the URL. In this case the only layer is called elevation:cded250k (as shown in the LAYERS parameter). If no layer is provided, then gdal_translate will fail and tell you as much. The URL required is what follows the WMS: prefix, above, and can be truncated after the LAYERS parameter part:

```
WMS:http://ows.geobase.ca/wms/geobase_en?SERVICE=WMS
     &VERSION=1.1.1&REQUEST=GetMap&LAYERS=elevation:cded250k
```

The other item you will need to consider is what size of output image you are after. If you leave it blank, it will try a best guess but seems to sometimes take as high a resolution as possible which may not be what you, or the service provider, really need.[23]

[23] With this particular server, my simple request, without a -outsize option, started to create an image that was 8947849 x 5965232 in size. I quit when the file had hit 95MB in size.

With this in mind, you can create a very simple request. In the following example, I use a country-wide layer instead of the elevation layer that we'll use in a moment:

```
WMS:http://ows.geobase.ca/wms/geobase_en?SERVICE=WMS \
     &VERSION=1.1.1&REQUEST=GetMap&LAYERS=elevation:cded250k
```

```
gdal_translate -outsize 1800 900  \
  "WMS:http://ows.geobase.ca/wms/geobase_en?SERVICE=WMS \
    &VERSION=1.1.1&REQUEST=GetMap&LAYERS=WMS-GeoBase \
    &SRS=EPSG:4269" wms_out1.tif
```

If you want to grab all the possible layers, you can remove the LAYERS parameter and include the -sds option in the command. This will query and save all layers (subdatasets) that the WMS provides. Provide an output filename and each layer will have an incremented number in the filename:

```
gdal_translate -outsize 300 200  \
```

```
             -projwin -124 54 -121 52 -sds  \
             "WMS:http://ows.geobase.ca/wms/geobase_en" \
             layer
```

This produces layer1, layer2, etc filenames. Obviously this might take a while and some layers may not cover the extent you provided in the -projwin option so they will be blank.

To translate only one layer, add the LAYERS= description to the WMS URL. This converts just the CDED elevation layer from the WMS and stores it at high resolution, in PNG format:

```
gdal_translate -outsize 3000 2000  \
               -projwin -124 54 -121 52  \
               -sds  \
               -of PNG \
               "WMS:http://ows.geobase.ca/wms/geobase_en \
                &LAYERS=elevation:cded250k" \
                layer_cded.png
```

The resulting image is shown in Figure 2.1, on the following page.

For more general information and usage examples see other chapters on raster data conversion and the gdal_translate command syntax, on page 119.

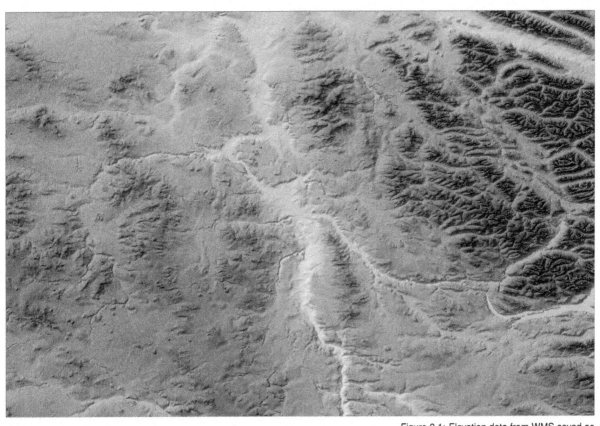

Figure 2.1: Elevation data from WMS saved as PNG

3

Report Vector Information - ogrinfo

Contents

In the following examples, we will be using the Natural Earth dataset mentioned previously in the Sample Data chapter, on page 13. As you try the examples, each command must be run from within the ne folder. We'll be looking at the shapefiles that came with the data.

The *ESRI Shapefile* format consists of three or more files, all with the same filename prefix, but different suffixes (.shp, .shx, .dbf). Referencing just the .shp file is enough for OGR to figure out what you mean. In addition, you can specify the parent folder name and OGR will find all the shapefiles within it.

List Supported Vector Formats

List the available formats that ogrinfo can access, by using the general option --formats. The results also tell whether GDAL/OGR can only read/open the format, or whether it can also write new layers in that format:

```
ogrinfo --formats

Supported Formats:
  -> "ESRI Shapefile" (read/write)
  -> "MapInfo File" (read/write)
  -> "UK .NTF" (readonly)
  ...
```

List Available Layers

List the **available layers** in a *datasource*, in this case shapefiles. In other formats, the datasource may be a file, folder, or database connection string. In the following example, it is a folder name:

```
ogrinfo 10m_cultural

INFO: Open of `10m_cultural/'
      using driver `ESRI Shapefile' successful.
1: ne_10m_admin_0_boundary_lines_disputed_areas (Line String)
2: ne_10m_admin_0_boundary_lines_land (Line String)
3: ne_10m_admin_0_boundary_lines_maritime_indicator (Line String)
4: ne_10m_admin_0_disputed_areas (Polygon)
5: ne_10m_admin_0_map_subunits (Polygon)
6: ne_10m_admin_0_map_units (Polygon)
7: ne_10m_admin_0_scale_rank_minor_islands (Polygon)
8: ne_10m_admin_1_states_provinces_lines_shp (Line String)
9: ne_10m_admin_1_states_provinces_shp (Polygon)
10: ne_10m_populated_places (Point)
11: ne_10m_urban_areas (Polygon)
```

List Layer Summary and Details

List **summary information about all the layers** in a datasource, in this case, all the shapefiles in the folder. By using the -so summary option with the -al all layers option, we keep the output manageable:

```
ogrinfo -so -al 10m_cultural
```

The result is over 500 lines of output, listing each layer, its attributes, geometry type, feature count, extent and more. Without the -so option it would have output all the individual feature information (attributes and geometry) as well.

List **all the features** of a given layer by adding the layer name to the datasource name:

```
ogrinfo 10m_cultural ne_10m_populated_places
```

This command will list every feature, every attribute and spew it out to the command prompt. This can be helpful if you want to push the resulting data through more filters and text processing commands like sed, grep, or awk or even out to web services and other scripts.

List **summary information about the layer** by adding the -so option. This shows all the attribute names, full extent of all features, projections, feature count, etc.:

```
ogrinfo -so 10m_cultural ne_10m_populated_places

INFO: Open of `10m_cultural'
    using driver `ESRI Shapefile' successful.

Layer name: ne_10m_populated_places
Geometry: Point
Feature Count: 7314
Extent: (-179.589979, -89.982894) - (179.383304, 82.483323)
Layer SRS WKT:
GEOGCS["GCS_WGS_1984",
```

```
        DATUM["WGS_1984",
            SPHEROID["WGS_1984",6378137.0,298.257223563]],
        PRIMEM["Greenwich",0.0],
        UNIT["Degree",0.0174532925199433]]
    SCALERANK: Integer (4.0)
    NATSCALE: Integer (4.0)
    LABELRANK: Integer (4.0)
    FEATURECLA: String (50.0)
    ...
```

Use SQL Query Syntax

Use a SQL-style -where clause option to return only the features
that meet the expression. In this case, only return the populated
places features that meet the criteria of having NAME = 'Shanghai':

```
ogrinfo  10m_cultural ne_10m_populated_places
        -where "NAME = 'Shanghai'"


...
Feature Count: 1
Extent: (-179.589979, -89.982894) - (179.383304, 82.483323)
...
OGRFeature(ne_10m_populated_places):6282
  SCALERANK (Integer) = 1
  NATSCALE (Integer) = 300
  LABELRANK (Integer) = 1
  FEATURECLA (String) = Admin-1 capital
  NAME (String) = Shanghai
  ...
  CITYALT (String) = (null)
  popDiff (Integer) = 1
  popPerc (Real) = 1.00000000000
  ls_gross (Integer) = 0
  POINT (121.434558819820154 31.218398311228327)
```

Building on the above, you can also query across all available layers,[24]
using the -al option and removing the specific layer name. Keep
the same -where syntax and it will try to use it on each layer. In

cases where a layer does not have the specific attribute, it will tell you, but will continue to process the other layers:

```
ERROR 1: 'NAME' not recognised as an available field.
```

[24] More recent versions of ogrinfo appear to not support this and will likely give FAILURE messages instead.

Select By FID or WHERE Clause

List all the first features in each layer in the folder, using the -fid option to specify which unique feature ID number you want to report on. Here we tell it to report all of the first ones. This is synonymous to using -where FID=1:

```
ogrinfo 10m_cultural -al -fid 1
```

Note that here we also used the -al option, though you can provide a layer name instead to reduce the results to one layer.

Use a full SQL-style query to restrict resulting features to a particular expression.

Using the -sql option gives you some of the same functionality as the -where clause option, but with the ability to perform a variety of other tasks, depending on what the datasource allows.[25] See OGR's SQL page for more description.[26]

[25] **Databases**
Normally ogrinfo builds its own SQL statement, but in some situations, when using the -sql option, it passes the statement directly to the datasource to be processed. This is mostly the case with database datasources (PostgreSQL, SQLite, etc.). OGR SQL allows SQL-like commands to pass to non-database datasources as well.

[26] OGR SQL: http://loc8.cc/ogr_sql

To return only details for two columns (SOV0NAME and NAME) from the places layer:

```
ogrinfo  10m_cultural -sql "SELECT SOV0NAME, NAME \
         FROM 'ne_10m_populated_places'"


...
SOV0NAME: String (100.0)
NAME: String (100.0)
OGRFeature(ne_10m_populated_places):0
  SOV0NAME (String) = Uruguay
  NAME (String) = Carmelo
  POINT (-58.29999210776765 -33.989619121538851)

OGRFeature(ne_10m_populated_places):1
```

```
SOV0NAME (String) = Uruguay
NAME (String) = San Jose de Mayo
POINT (-56.709985800795152 -34.349958883910062)
...
```

Rename Output Field Using SQL Query

A basic query can also be used to rename one of the output fields with an alias.[27] In this case we select the SOV0NAME column and present it with the alias COUNTRY instead:

```
ogrinfo  10m_cultural -sql "SELECT SOV0NAME AS COUNTRY \
             FROM 'ne_10m_populated_places'"


...
COUNTRY: String (100.0)
OGRFeature(ne_10m_populated_places):0
  COUNTRY (String) = Uruguay
  POINT (-58.29999210776765 -33.989619121538851)

OGRFeature(ne_10m_populated_places):1
  COUNTRY (String) = Uruguay
  POINT (-56.709985800795152 -34.349958883910062)
...
```

More SQL Examples

More advanced SQL can also be used, including calculations and aggregate functions. In this example we do a feature count limited by a WHERE clause, returning the number of entries in the layer that are within Canada:

```
ogrinfo 10m_cultural -sql "SELECT count(*) \
        FROM 'ne_10m_populated_places' WHERE SOV0NAME = 'Canada'"

INFO: Open of `10m_cultural'
      using driver `ESRI Shapefile' successful.

Layer name: ne_10m_populated_places
Geometry: Point
```

```
Feature Count: 1
Layer SRS WKT:
(unknown)
COUNT_*: Integer (0.0)
OGRFeature(ne_10m_populated_places):0
  COUNT_* (Integer) = 256
```

The result is shown in the last line, where the COUNT_* variable is 256.

Additional commands include SQL ORDER BY, GROUP BY, math functions, JOIN operations and more:

```
ogrinfo 10m_cultural -sql "SELECT c.NAME, p.NAME \
        FROM 'ne_10m_admin_1_states_provinces_shp' c
        LEFT JOIN 'ne_10m_populated_places' p ON p.SOV0NAME = c.SOV0NAME"
```

Apply Spatial Filters

A spatial filter can be applied, returning only those records that touch or fall inside the provided bounding box coordinates.[28] Use -spat minx miny maxx maxy syntax and -so to only give a summary count of the number of features within the given area:

```
ogrinfo 10m_cultural ne_10m_populated_places
        -spat -122 50 -120 54 -so

Layer name: ne_10m_populated_places
Geometry: Point
Feature Count: 2
Extent: (-179.589979, -89.982894) - (179.383304, 82.483323)
Layer SRS WKT:
...
```

You can apply a spatial filter across several layers at once by adding more layer names or using the -al all layers option. Using a grep command is also handy for summarising the results of such a function. In this case, eleven layers are queried and the number of features within each layer (that meet our spatial filter requirements) are reported:

[28] The -spat option **does not** cut or break features that may extend beyond the borders of the rectangle—it simply returns the full feature—e.g. it won't trim or break input features into new parts if it overlaps the region rectangle provided.

```
ogrinfo 10m_cultural -spat -122 50 -120 54 \
  -so -al | grep Feature\ Count

Feature Count: 0
Feature Count: 0
Feature Count: 0
Feature Count: 0
Feature Count: 3
Feature Count: 3
Feature Count: 1
Feature Count: 1
Feature Count: 4
Feature Count: 2
Feature Count: 2
```

Query GeoNames Gazetteer

Building on the other examples in this chapter, here are a few more that use the GeoNames dataset presented in the Sample Data section, on page 13. These examples use only the Canadian portion of the global dataset in order to keep size manageable—but the full dataset is available for free. Regardless, the goal is to show patterns for extracting valuable information using OGR commands.

First, list entries in the datafile. Because the default name of the Canadian GeoNames files is CA.txt—OGR does not automatically discover its format. As it is a tab delimited file, it can be opened with the CSV format, but it has to be explicitly told to (either by renaming the file or specifying the driver prefix):

```
ogrinfo CSV:CA.txt
INFO: Open of `CSV:CA.txt'
    using driver `CSV' successful.

Layer name: CA
Geometry: Point
Feature Count: 308427
Extent: (-141.005420, 41.683380) - (-48.500000, 83.122240)
```

...

Next, using `ogrinfo` with the `-spat` option, reduce the set to only
those within a certain spatial extent/bounding box rectangle:

```
ogrinfo CSV:CA.txt -spat -122 40 -120 50 CA

INFO: Open of `CSV:CA.txt'
     using driver `CSV' successful.

Layer name: CA
Geometry: Point
Feature Count: 6181
Extent: (-121.991870, 48.999680) - (-120.002410, 59.983380)
```

Note that the `Extent` that is returned only includes the extent of
the points that fell within your rectangle provided by `-spat` and the
count of points is only 6,181 out of 308,427.

Return a particular town name by using the `-where` option:

```
ogrinfo CSV:CA.txt -where 'NAME = "Straffordville"' CA

Layer name: CA
Geometry: Point
Feature Count: 1
Extent: (-80.783000, 42.750100) - (-80.783000, 42.750100)
```

Return multiple matches by using the `IN` operator in the `WHERE`
clause:

```
ogrinfo CSV:CA.txt
  -where 'NAME IN ("Straffordville","Williams Lake")' CA

INFO: Open of `CSV:CA.txt'
     using driver `CSV' successful.

Layer name: CA
Geometry: Point
Feature Count: 22
Extent: (-132.269230, 42.750100) - (-63.051040, 68.549980)
```

```
Layer SRS WKT:
...
```

Use multiple columns in the WHERE clause, in this case to only show the towns defined by the feature code column. One of the towns is so small it is referred to as an AREA whereas the other is a populated place (PPL):

```
ogrinfo CSV:CA.txt \
  -where 'NAME IN ("Straffordville","Williams Lake") \
  AND FEATCODE IN ("AREA","PPL")' CA

Layer name: CA
Geometry: Point
Feature Count: 2
Extent: (-122.144510, 42.750100) - (-80.783000, 52.141530)
...
```

4

Web Services - Retrieving Vectors (WFS)

These features require GDAL [**v1.8+**].

OGR utilities are able to interact with online web mapping servers that publish their vector data using the WFS protocol. There is much that can be done, including transactional WFS, but these examples are only meant to get you started. See the online documentation for the OGR WFS driver for more details.[29]

[29] OGR WFS: http://loc8.cc/ogr_wfs

Using ogrinfo to Get Capabilities of a WFS

There are three components in a WFS request to consider—here is a simple example that returns the layers in typical ogrinfo style:

```
ogrinfo -ro "WFS:http://cgns.nrcan.gc.ca/wfsu/cubeserv.cgi? \
            service=wfs&datastore=cgns"

INFO: Open of `WFS:http://cgns.nrcan.gc.ca/wfsu/cubeserv.cgi?
service=wfs&datastore=cgns'
      using driver `WFS' successful.
1: cw:CGNS_CODES
2: cw:GEONAMES (Point)
```

The -ro option opens the connection as read-only to prevent ogrinfo from trying to open it in read/write mode. For the purposes of this demo, it just keeps OGR from giving an ERROR when it tests to see if it's an editable data source.

The second thing to notice is the WFS: prefix which tells OGR the type of data source we are connecting to.[30]

[30] Using a prefix forces OGR to use a particular driver to open a data source. This approach can be especially useful if the filename of a data source may not follow normal naming conventions—for example, a CSV file with a non .csv extension.

The third element in this example is the URL to the WFS. WFS URLs are often more complicated than our example. If using a GeoServer-based WFS, the URLs often take the form of:

```
http://localhost:8080/geoserver/wfs
```

Similar to all ogrinfo commands, you can retrieve more information by providing layer names, filters and more. Those examples are provided elsewhere in the ogrinfo sections of this book.

There is one additional command that is worth knowing for the OGR WFS driver. Those who are used to working with WFS/WMS, etc. are familiar with using GetCapabilities requests to get detailed service information. This includes more than just layer names, but a full response according the WFS specification.

To retrieve a full GetCapabilities document, there is a hidden layer name you can provide that will output all the details (URL broken onto two lines for readability):

```
ogrinfo -ro "WFS:http://cgns.nrcan.gc.ca/wfsu/cubeserv.cgi? \
             service=wfs&datastore=cgns" WFSGetCapabilities

Layer name: WFSGetCapabilities
Geometry: None
Feature Count: 1
Layer SRS WKT:
(unknown)
content: String (0.0)
OGRFeature(WFSGetCapabilities):0
  content (String) = <?xml version="1.0" encoding="UTF-8"?>
```

```
<WFS_Capabilities version="1.1.0" xmlns="...
<ows:ServiceIdentification>
 <ows:Title>
  Canadian Geographical Names Service Web Feature Service
 </ows:Title>
 <ows:Abstract>The geographical names WFS allows a...
 ...
```

Note that at the beginning of the response is the standard OGR output, so if you are planning to re-use the document, there is a little bit of cleaning required to remove those first ten or so header lines.

5

Translate Rasters - gdal_translate

Contents

GDAL is often best known for its ability to convert/translate between various **raster** data formats using the gdal_translate command. Along with this is the ability to define the coordinate systems, remove bands and adjust output size.[31]

[31] For converting between **vector** formats, use the ogr2ogr command in the Translate Vectors - ogr2ogr chapter, on page 63.

The following examples use the raster data downloaded from the Natural Earth Data website described in the Sample Data chapter on page 13 and shown in Figure 5.1, on the following page.

Figure 5.1: Natural Earth raster world map image

List Supported Raster Formats

Run the gdalinfo command with the --formats option to see a list of the raster data formats that your version of GDAL/OGR supports. The result also shows whether the format can be used for read and/or write[32].

[32] 'ro' is read-only driver; 'rw' is read or write; 'rw+' is read, write and update. A 'v' is appended for formats supporting virtual IO.

Results will vary depending on what formats were enabled during the build of your GDAL installation:

```
gdalinfo --formats

Supported Formats:
  VRT (rw+v): Virtual Raster
  GTiff (rw+v): GeoTIFF
  NITF (rw+v): National Imagery Transmission Format
  RPFTOC (rov): Raster Product Format TOC format
  HFA (rw+v): Erdas Imagine Images (.img)
  SAR_CEOS (rov): CEOS SAR Image
  ...
```

Convert Raster File Between Formats

In this example, gdal_translate is used to convert a GeoTIFF format file into a JPEG format. This is done simply by providing the input and output filenames, along with an output format option

(-of):

```
gdal_translate -of JPEG NE1_50M_SR_W.tif ne1_50m.jpg

Input file size is 10800, 5400
0...10...20...30...40...50...60...70...80...90...100 - done.
```

Extract a Single Band from a Raster

The gdal_translate command can be used to select specific bands from the source raster:

```
gdal_translate -b 1 NE1_50M_SR_W.tif ne1_50m_band1.tif

Input file size is 10800, 5400
0...10...20...30...40...50...60...70...80...90...100 - done.
```

Here, gdal_translate uses its band select option (-b n) to select which band number (n) to read/write during the translation operation. By default it will normally translate all input bands. No output format is specified, so it will use GeoTIFF by default

See Figure 5.2 for the results.

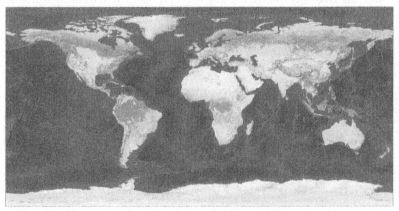

Figure 5.2: Band one extracted from the Natural Earth raster world map image

Listing the file sizes, or running gdalinfo against the output file will show that the file has only a single band and is 1/3 of the size due to the other two bands being ignored during translation:

```
167M 17 Dec  2010 NE1_50M_SR_W.tif
56M 16 Jan 22:31 ne1_50m_band1.tif
```

Resize a Raster During Translation

The -outsize option allows a raster to grow or shrink depending on the desired number of rows/columns or based on a relative percentage (%) growth. Both the x and y size values are specified in the command:

```
gdal_translate -outsize 20% 20% NE1_50M_SR_W.tif \
               ne1_50m_20pct.tif
```

This will reduce the output size to 20% of the input. In this case, 20% of the input size equates to an output of 2160 x 1080 pixels.

Expand an image by providing an outsize of greater than 100%:

```
gdal_translate -outsize 200% 200% NE1_50M_SR_W.tif \
               ne1_50m_200pct.tif
```

Clip a Portion of a Raster During Translation

There are two ways to define subsets of a raster when doing a translation. First is by specifying the raw row and column numbers for the range desired, using the -srcwin option and a upper left to lower right bounding list of pixel coordinates.

The resulting output image from these commands is shown in Figure 5.3, on the facing page.

The source file has dimensions of 10800x5400, so the coordinate range of interest must fall within those dimensions:

```
gdal_translate -srcwin 0 0 2500 2500 NE1_50M_SR_W.tif \
               ne1_50m_sub.tif
```

The second method to define a subset is by using the -projwin projected window method, where you provide a list of coordinates in the form of the projected coordinate system assigned to the raster.

Figure 5.3: Subset of Natural Earth raster world map image

In the case of our dataset, the coordinate system is latitude / longitude.

When running the command, it will tell you how it computes the pixel row/columns to use for the given projected window:

```
gdal_translate -projwin -180 90 -120 49 NE1_50M_SR_W.tif \
            ne1_50m_sub2.tif


Input file size is 10800, 5400
Computed -srcwin 0 0 1800 1230 from projected window.
0...10...20...30...40...50...60...70...80...90...100 - done.
```

Convert an ASCII Grid / Text File to Raster File

Gridded text can be used as input into a GDAL raster.

In this case, a grid refers to a *regularly* spaced set of coordinates and data values.[33]

[33] There are at least two different formats for text-based grid files. The first is shown here, another (XYZ format) is shown in the next section.

A basic text format of gridded data would look similar to the following, where each row represents a row in the raster and each column a column in the raster:

```
100 100 100 100 100
200 100 150 150 100
200 150 200 200 150
200 200 200 200 200
200 200 150 100 150
```

This would represent a 5x5 grid. Notice there are no blank or missing values; if there were then this would not be a *regular* grid (more on *irregular* grids below).

Figure 5.4, on the next page shows what this 5x5 grid looks like when rendered with shades of grey assigned to each value above.

In order for GDAL to read the above dataset, it needs a little more information added to the file. It needs to know the number of rows and columns, where they are positioned in space (lower left corner x and y coordinates) and cell/pixel size in units on the ground (i.e. metres, feet, degrees). Here is a sample header to add to the top of the grid text file:

```
ncols        5
nrows        5
xllcorner    -121
yllcorner    52
cellsize     1
100 100 100 100 100
200 100 150 150 100
200 150 200 200 150
200 200 200 200 200
```

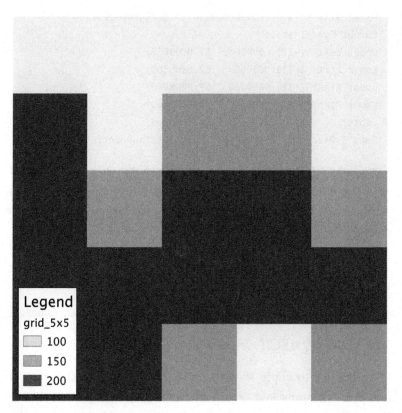

Figure 5.4: Example rendering of ASCII grid, 5x5 cells

```
200 200 150 100 150
```

The result covers an area of 5 by 5 degrees in size, with each cell being 1x1 degree.

The gdalinfo command can now read grid.txt and display the following information:

```
gdalinfo grid.txt

Driver: AAIGrid/Arc/Info ASCII Grid
Files: grid.txt
Size is 5, 5
Coordinate System is `'
Origin = (-121.000000000000000,57.000000000000000)
```

```
Pixel Size = (1.000000000000000,-1.000000000000000)
Corner Coordinates:
Upper Left  (-121.0000000,  57.0000000)
Lower Left  (-121.0000000,  52.0000000)
Upper Right (-116.0000000,  57.0000000)
Lower Right (-116.0000000,  52.0000000)
Center      (-118.5000000,  54.5000000)
Band 1 Block=5x1 Type=Int32, ColorInterp=Undefined
```

Now that we have added the header information to grid.txt, it can be converted to a raster. Specify the output format (-of) or leave it blank to assume the default GeoTIFF output format. This example uses GeoTIFF:

```
gdal_translate grid.txt grid.tif

Input file size is 5, 5
0...10...20...30...40...50...60...70...80...90...100 - done.
```

Convert XYZ ASCII Grid Data to Raster File

The previous example shows how to use gridded text data with rows and columns laid out in the text file. In *gridded XYZ data*, each cell is put on a separate line in the text file. The X and Y column values are specified, then the Z (or whatever third value that number represents):

```
x  y  z
1  1  200
1  2  300
1  3  100
2  1  100
2  2  200
```

The previous text grid file (grid.txt) we used can be converted into XYZ format, to help show what the data should look like. Specify -of XYZ as the output format:

```
gdal_translate -of XYZ grid.txt grid.xyz
```

Here is a subset of the results, in XYZ data format. Note the coordinates are computed by `gdal_translate` automatically and dumped into the list. The coordinates, by default, represent the location of the centre of each cell:

```
-120.5 56.5 100
-119.5 56.5 100
-118.5 56.5 100
-117.5 56.5 100
-116.5 56.5 100
-120.5 55.5 200
-119.5 55.5 100
-118.5 55.5 150
...
```

Mimic this format in a text file and you can easily convert to a raster, without any header information about cell sizes or coordinate start points.[34]

[34] The coordinates must be uniform and regular or `gdal_translate` will throw an error complaining about them. It checks the distance between the first two coordinates and expects the next one to be the same difference.

Convert the XYZ data back into another format, for example as a GeoTIFF using:

```
gdal_translate grid.xyz newgrid.tif
```

Convert Irregular Data to a Grid

To convert irregular ASCII grid data requires a few discrete steps, but is not onerous if you know the right tools.

See Figure 5.5, on the following page for an example of what the vector source data looks like and the resulting raster interpolation.

There are three steps required to convert the irregular grid to a raster:

1. Convert XYZ data into CSV text

If the source data is in a grid text format with rows and columns, then convert it to the XYZ output format with `gdal_translate` as shown in the previous example.

Figure 5.5: Irregular grid points with underlying interpolated raster using gdal_grid

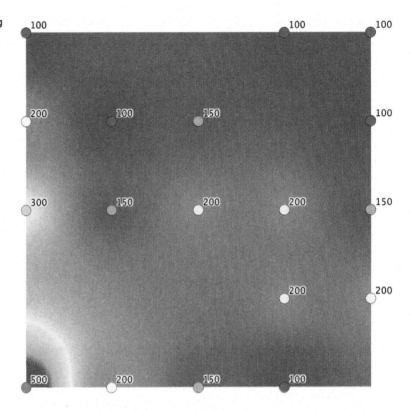

Once in an XYZ format, change the space delimiters to commas (tabs and semicolon also supported). This is easily done on the command line using a tool like sed or manually in a text editor:

```
sed 's/ /,/g' grid.xyz > grid.csv
```

The resulting CSV file looks like:

```
-120.5,56.5,100
-119.5,56.5,100
-118.5,56.5,100
-117.5,56.5,100
...
```

2. Create a virtual format header file

Step 3 will require access to the CSV grid data in an OGR supported format, so we create a simple XML text file (known as a VRT) that can then be referred to as a vector datasource with any of the OGR tools.

Create the file grid.vrt with the following content; note the pointers to the source CSV file and the fields which are automatically discerned from the CSV file on-the-fly:

```
<OGRVRTDataSource>
    <OGRVRTLayer name="grid">
        <SrcDataSource>grid.csv</SrcDataSource>
        <GeometryType>wkbPoint</GeometryType>
        <LayerSRS>WGS84</LayerSRS>
        <GeometryField separator=","
                       encoding="PointFromColumns"
                       x="field_1" y="field_2" z="field_3" />
    </OGRVRTLayer>
</OGRVRTDataSource>
```

If the first row of the grid.csv file includes custom field names, e.g. X, Y, Z, then substitute them for the field_1, field_2 and field_3 settings above.

3. Convert using gdal_grid

Now for the following step, convert this OGR vector VRT and CSV format into a GDAL raster format, while also interpolating any "missing" points in the grid. Various options are available for interpolating. See the gdal_grid command syntax, on page 179 for more information—a minimal example is shown here using all the defaults:

```
gdal_grid -zfield field_3 -l grid grid.vrt newgrid.tif
```

The output product will fill in any holes in the source grid. Several algorithms are available; the default uses the *"Inverse distance to a power"* option. The input layer name is provided by the -l option.

You'll find detailed information for **CSV File & VRT XML Formats** on page 287.

Georeference using Ground Control Points (GCP)

Georeferencing a raster can be done using gdal_translate and the -gcp option. To apply a true transformation to the raster, it can then be processed with gdalwarp (see Transform Rasters - gdalwarp, on page 71 for examples).

Using a basic world map image, this example assigns four ground control points (GCP) so that applications can position it geographically. The map image being used has no previous georeferencing or coordinate system defined for it—think of it as a screenshot or a plain old digital photo. It's using the Natural Earth raster map, reduced to 10% of original size and converted to JPEG format. See the Natural Earth Data section, on page 13 in Part I: Getting Started to access the original raster file.

The gdal_translate command has many options; only the most basic are shown here. See the gdal_translate chapter on page 119 for more details. Multiple GCP can be assigned by repeating the -gcp option, each time with a different set of values. Each set of four values represent the X and Y pixel numbers and their matching easting/longitude and northing/latitude coordinates.

In this example, each of the four corners of the image are assigned a GCP, and the result is saved into the new output file with the GCP recorded internally. The image dimensions are 1080x540:

```
gdal_translate -gcp 0 0 -180 90 \
               -gcp 0 540 -180 -90 \
               -gcp 1080 0 180 90 \
               -gcp 1080 540 180 -90 \
               ne1_nonreg.jpg ne1_reg.tif
```

Check the output result to see how its metadata looks:

```
gdalinfo ne1_reg.tif
```

```
Driver: GTiff/GeoTIFF
Files: ne1_reg.tif
Size is 1080, 540
Coordinate System is `'
GCP Projection =
GCP[  0]: Id=1, Info=
          (0,0) -> (-180,90,0)
GCP[  1]: Id=2, Info=
          (0,540) -> (-180,-90,0)
GCP[  2]: Id=3, Info=
          (1080,0) -> (180,90,0)
GCP[  3]: Id=4, Info=
          (1080,540) -> (180,-90,0)
Image Structure Metadata:
  INTERLEAVE=PIXEL
Corner Coordinates:
Upper Left  (    0.0,     0.0)
Lower Left  (    0.0,   540.0)
Upper Right ( 1080.0,     0.0)
Lower Right ( 1080.0,   540.0)
Center      (  540.0,   270.0)
```

You can see how the transformation parameters are stored as metadata in the file.

Modify the conversion to also provide a coordinate system reference, by adding the -a_srs option. [35]

In this case we specify using the EPSG SRS ID number for WGS 84, latitude/longitude:

```
gdal_translate -a_srs epsg:4326 -gcp 0 0 -180 90 -gcp ...
```

To actually warp the image to use the GCP and generate a new, fully georeferenced raster, run:

```
gdalwarp ne1_reg.tif ne1_warped.tif
```

You'll find detailed information for gdalwarp in the Transform Rasters - gdalwarp chapter on page 205.

[35] Can't remember all these EPSG and SRS numbers? See the http://spatialreference.org or http://epsg.io sites for more information.

6

Translate Vectors - ogr2ogr

Contents

OGR conversion commands enable processing of **vector** datasets. Data can be transformed between coordinate systems, layers dropped, and records filtered or queried.

The following examples use the vector data downloaded from the Natural Earth Data website described in the Sample Data chapter on page 13.[36]

[36] For converting between **raster** formats, see the Translate Rasters - gdal_translate chapter, on page 49.

List Supported Vector Formats

Run the `ogr2ogr` command with the `--formats` option to see a list of the vector data formats that your version of GDAL/OGR supports. The result also shows whether the format can be used for read and/or write.

Results will vary depending on what formats were enabled during the build of your GDAL installation:

```
ogr2ogr --formats
Supported Formats:
  -> "ESRI Shapefile" (read/write)
  -> "MapInfo File" (read/write)
  -> "UK .NTF" (readonly)
  -> "SDTS" (readonly)
  -> "TIGER" (read/write)
  -> "S57" (read/write)
  ...
```

Convert Vector File Between Formats

In this example, ogr2ogr is used to convert a Shapefile into a GML file. This is done by providing the output data filename and input filename, along with an output format option (-f):

```
ogr2ogr -f GML pop_places.gml ne_110m_populated_places.shp
```

Check the output using ogrinfo to ensure it translated properly:

```
ogrinfo pop_places.gml -al -so

Had to open data source read-only.
INFO: Open of `pop_places.gml'
      using driver `GML' successful.

Layer name: ne_110m_populated_places
Geometry: Point
Feature Count: 326
Extent: (-175.2205, -41.2999) - (179.2166, 64.1500)
Layer SRS WKT:
(unknown)
Geometry Column = geometryProperty
fid: String (0.0)
SCALERANK: Integer (4.0)
```

```
NATSCALE: Integer (4.0)
LABELRANK: Integer (4.0)
...
```

Extract a Single Layer from a Vector Datasource

Many OGR datasources can have multiple layers. In the above example, there is only one layer in the source shapefile, so it was used by default. If there had been more than one layer, all of them would have been available since GML can handle multiple layers.

By specifying a layer name, you can control more precisely what will be in the output file.[37]

[37] If this was a database data source, the layer would be the name of a table/view instead of a file or folder name.

In this example, we'll use the main Natural Earth folder as the data source and specify one of the shapefile names as the layer:

```
ogr2ogr single.shp ne/110m_cultural ne_110m_populated_places
```

This takes the `ne_110m_populated_places` layer from within the `ne/110m_cultural/` folder and creates a new file called `single.shp`.[38]

[38] When specifying input and output names with `ogr2ogr`, the **output** name always comes first.

Convert Multiple Layers Into a New Datasource

To build on the above conversion we specify additional layer names at the end of the command. GML supports multiple layers of different types. Here we convert polygon and point layers, from two different shapefiles, and save them in the output GML:

```
ogr2ogr -f GML various.gml ne/110m_cultural \
              ne_110m_admin_0_countries \
              ne_110m_populated_places
```

Confirm the output created multiple layers:

```
ogrinfo various.gml
Had to open data source read-only.
INFO: Open of `various.gml'
      using driver `GML' successful.
1: ne_110m_admin_0_countries (Polygon)
```

```
    2: ne_110m_populated_places (Point)
```

Extract Features Using a SQL Query

There are many options for querying a vector dataset and only re-
trieving/converting features of interest. This can be done to create
a new file in a different format, or to act as a filter process into a
new file of the same format.

As usual, the default output format is ESRI Shapefile.

To define filter criteria, use the -where or -sql options. There are
differences between the two, but for this example use the first one
to identify a *where* clause:

```
ogr2ogr -where 'NAME="London"' output.shp \
                ne_110m_populated_places.shp
```

[39] If you have trouble with your query syntax, pay special attention to how you are quoting the field name and values.

The result is a single point matching the criteria.[39]

Filter Features Based On Location

In addition to filtering using field values, you can also query the input data using a spatial filter. You define a rectangular area (south-
western and northeastern most points) and OGR will select only
these features that are within or touching that area:

```
ogr2ogr -spat 0 0 125 40 output_filter.shp \
                ne_110m_populated_places.shp
```

See that the output[40] makes sense:

```
$ ogrinfo output.shp -al -so
  INFO: Open of `output.shp'
      using driver `ESRI Shapefile' successful.

Layer name: output
Geometry: Point
Feature Count: 116
Extent: (1.220811, 0.318605) - (121.448046, 39.930838)
  ..
```

[40] Notice that the Extent is smaller than our in-put bounding box. This extent represents all the features that were in the input file and fell within the bounding box. The -spat option does not clip or intersect to create new features in the output for the bounding box.

Reproject Vector Data

You can easily transform your vector data between spatial reference systems and projections. The sample dataset we have been using is stored in latitude/longitude and can be projected to any GDAL supported spatial reference system (SRS).

There are three particular options to use for handling SRS:

- -a_srs allows you to assign a SRS in the case where it was not already defined in the source data.
- -s_srs allows you to override an existing source SRS.
- -t_srs specifies the *target* SRS

Using EPSG[41] codes is the simplest way to define the projection:

```
ogr2ogr -t_srs "epsg:3035" \
    country_3035.shp ne_110m_admin_0_countries.shp
```

Figure 6.1, on the next page shows the result of projecting the ne_110m_admin_0_countries.shp file to EPSG 3035.

[41] For finding EPSG numbers, use the http://spatialreference.org website to look up various options. There is also a file named epsg in your GDAL/OGR installation folders which has the same details.

Setup GDAL_DATA Variable

The last example will fail if certain GDAL configuration files are not found by the system. If this happens, the solution is to define the GDAL_DATA environment variable that points to the location of the GDAL support files.

The appropriate GDAL folder may be in:

- Mac: /Library/Frameworks/GDAL.framework/Resources/gdal/
- Linux: /usr/share/gdal/ or /usr/local/share/gdal
- Windows: C:\OSGeo4W\share\gdal

Setup PROJ_LIB Variable

GDAL/OGR also uses the PROJ library for doing projections and ogr2ogr must be able to find them to operate properly. If things don't work out of the box, you can set the PROJ_LIB variable to point

Figure 6.1: Projected country data

to the proper directory. Depending on your system, the appropriate
directory may be similar to:

- Mac: `/Library/Frameworks/PROJ.framework/Resources/proj/`
- Linux: `/usr/share/proj/` or `/usr/local/share/proj`
- Windows: `C:\OSGeo4W\share\proj`

These environment variables can be used together to solve GDAL/OGR
issues. A Linux/Mac example is shown below. Windows users
would use the `set` command instead of `export`:

```
export GDAL_DATA=
  /Library/Frameworks/GDAL.framework/Versions/1.9/Resources/gdal/
export PROJ_LIB=
  /Library/Frameworks/PROJ.framework/Versions/4/unix/lib/
```

On Windows you can also use the system settings to permanently
set these environment variables.

7

Transform Rasters - gdalwarp

Contents

Transform and warp a raster

The `gdalwarp` command can be used to reproject rasters from one coordinate system to another. For example, from lat/lon into UTM projection:

```
gdalwarp -t_srs epsg:26910 ne1_clip.tif ne1_utm.tif
```

The command reads the **source coordinate system** from the original raster. The **target system** is manually specified, in this case using the `-t_srs` option, and the EPSG code number for UTM Zone 10 projection (26910).

Because UTM is intended for a limited region, a subset of our global raster example was needed. First clip out a section of the raster, using `gdal_translate`:

```
gdal_translate -projwin -124 58 -118 49 NE1_50M_SR_W.tif ne1_clip.tif

Input file size is 10800, 5400
Computed -srcwin 1680 960 180 270 from projected window.
0...10...20...30...40...50...60...70...80...90...100 - done.
```

Then use gdalwarp to perform the transform with the above options:

```
gdalwarp -t_srs epsg:26910 ne1_clip.tif ne1_utm.tif

Creating output file that is 132P x 305L.
Processing input file ne1_clip.tif.
0...10...20...30...40...50...60...70...80...90...100 - done.
```

Warp a Raster By Specifying Input and Output Projections

When the source raster does not already include coordinate system metadata, this information must be specified at the time of warping/reprojecting the raster.

In the following example, -s_srs is used to define the input raster's SRS and -t_srs specifies the target SRS for the output. This is similar to the previous example, except the raster doesn't already have an SRS defined:

```
gdalwarp -s_srs epsg:4326 -t_srs epsg:26910 \
        ne1_clip.tif ne1_utm.tif
```

Assigning a Spatial Reference System to a Raster

Assign an SRS to a raster using the gdal_translate command with the -a_srs option. This creates a new raster, encoding the metadata needed by other GDAL utilities:

```
gdal_translate -a_srs epsg:4326 \
            ne1_clip.tif ne1_clip_4326.tif
```

With the SRS encoded in the new raster, other GDAL utilities can operate on it without the need for the -s_srs option.

Transform Raster with GCP to Warped Output

As shown in a previous chapter (Georeference using Ground Control Points (GCP) on page 60), ground control points can be easily added to any raster file using gdal_translate. Once the points have been added to the metadata of the raster, the gdalwarp command can simply be run to create the new file with complete georeferencing/warping.

In this example, the GCP are manually provided:

```
gdal_translate -gcp 0 0 -180 90 \
               -gcp 0 540 -180 -90 \
               -gcp 1080 0 180 90 \
               -gcp 1080 540 180 -90 \
                ne1_nonreg.jpg ne1_reg.tif


gdalwarp ne1_reg.tif ne1_warped.tif
```

8

Create Raster Overviews - gdaladdo

Contents

Warning

Be careful not to try to add overviews to rasters that are being viewed/edited by other software, as it can, theoretically,
corrupt your data if there is a conflict. It is always wise to
have a backup of your raster before applying any overviews,
or else use the external option described here.

The `gdaladdo` (add overviews) command *builds or rebuilds overview
images* for a raster. This can be a lifesaver—it helps create subset
views of the data at predefined scales. Overview levels are reduced
resolution versions of the source data, allowing lower resolution
rasters to be retrieved when higher detail is not needed. Overviews
can be built internally or in an external file.

Using overviews reduces the amount of processing and memory needed to render rasters in a client application such as QGIS.[42] If overviews are available, QGIS will use them automatically. The full resolution images are still available as you zoom in, but otherwise, the client application only shows what can be reasonably discerned on the screen. The outcome is faster loading and faster interaction.

For full usage description, see the gdaladdo command examples, or see below for the quickest way to get started using the command. The SPOT imagery sample data is used for examples in this chapter.

Create A Quick Set of Overviews

> **Tip**
>
> To follow along with the same data in these examples, use the GeoBase SPOT Satellite Imagery described in Part I Sample Data, on page 13—specifically the panchromatic image called *IMAGERY.TIF* found in the folder with the suffix "A".

The only required options needed are the overview levels to be created. The levels must be **integer** values that represent fractions of the source/full resolution. A set of square values is often recommended. Level values are specified in a list and determine how many levels are created. In this example, we create four levels at reduced resolutions of 1/2 through 1/16:

```
gdaladdo IMAGERY.TIF  2 4 8 16
```

This produces four overview levels with the following resolutions:

```
Full: 12,000 x 12,000
2 - 6,000 x 6,000
4 - 3,000 x 3,000
8 - 1,500 x 1,500
16 - 750 x 750
```

As you can see, creating overviews much higher than the 16 level on this image will have negligible impact on visualisation as the output resolution of the image will be less than 750 x 750 pixels - likely not as useful for most applications on a normal resolution screen.

Note that overviews are usually never accessed directly by a user, rather imagery libraries can interrogate the image and use the overviews as it sees fit. In the next example we will check to see what overviews are available in a raster.

List Existing Overviews

The gdalinfo command (not gdaladdo) will list all the overview levels that are available in any given dataset:

```
gdalinfo IMAGERY.TIF


..

Band 1 Block=12000x1 Type=Byte, ColorInterp=Gray
Overviews: 6000x6000, 3000x3000, 1500x1500, 750x750
```

The output confirms the results of our previous example.

Remove Overviews

Overviews can be easily removed from a raster using the -clean option:

```
gdaladdo -clean IMAGERY.TIF
```

Confirm by running the previous example (using gdalinfo) against the file to see that no overviews are listed. As shown in the next section, you can remove an external overview by simply deleting the .ovr file.

Create External Overviews

In cases where you do not want to modify the source raster, you can have gdaladdo put the overview data into a corresponding external file. This is particularly useful if you have a dataset that you cannot edit for various reasons.

To force external overviews, use the -ro *read-only* flag, and it will create a .ovr file in the same folder:

```
gdaladdo -ro IMAGERY.TIF 2 4 8 16
0...10...20...30...40...50...60...70...80...90...100 - done.

ls IMAGERY.TIF

 46M   IMAGERY.TIF.ovr
230M   IMAGERY.TIF
```

To remove an external overview, you can simply delete the .ovr file.

Tweaking Output of Overview Algorithms

There are multiple resampling algorithms available for computing overviews for different purposes. Some are better than others at, for example, displaying continuous surface data, and others may be more suitable for your satellite imagery.

The algorithms available include: nearest, average, average_magphase, cubic, gauss, and mode. See the complete gdaladdo command examples for more details.

The default algorithm is nearest, but average is the next most popular method. Experimentation is encouraged, especially when output is going to be through a web map with reduced colour map availability.

Select the average algorithm and re-run the earlier command:

```
gdaladdo -r average IMAGERY.TIF 2 4 8 16
```

If you compare the various outputs you will see that some may look different than others. As some of the results can be subjective, depending on your objective, always take some time to make sure they are what you are after. Note, however, that desktop GIS software may also resample imagery while drawing to the screen. Sometimes there are options in the software to disable resampling so you can see it unadulterated.

9

Create Tile Map Structure - gdal2tiles

Contents

> **Tip**
>
> This is a Python script that needs to be run against "new generation" Python GDAL bindings [**v1.7+**]

Tiles in a Tile Map Server (TMS) context are basically raster map data that's broken into tiny pre-rendered tiles for maximum web client loading efficiency. GDAL, with Python, can chop up your input raster into the folder/file name and numbering structures that TMS compliant clients expect.

The bonus with this utility is that it also creates a basic web mapping application that you can start using right away.

The script is designed to use georeferenced rasters, however, any raster should also work with the right options. The (georeferenced) Natural Earth raster dataset is used in the first examples, with a non-georeferenced raster at the end.

There are many options to tweak the output and setup of the map services; see the complete gdal2tiles chapter on page 167 for more information.

Minimal TMS Generation

At the bare minimum an input file is needed:

```
gdal2tiles.py NE1_50M_SR_W.tif
Generating Base Tiles:
0...10...20...30...40...50...60...70...80...90...100 - done.
Generating Overview Tiles:
0...10...20...30...40...50...60...70...80...90...100 - done.
```

The output created is the same name as the input file, and include an array of sub-folders and sample web pages:

```
NE1_50M_SR_W
NE1_50M_SR_W/0
NE1_50M_SR_W/0/0
NE1_50M_SR_W/0/0/0.png
NE1_50M_SR_W/1
...
NE1_50M_SR_W/4/9/7.png
NE1_50M_SR_W/4/9/8.png
NE1_50M_SR_W/4/9/9.png
NE1_50M_SR_W/googlemaps.html
NE1_50M_SR_W/openlayers.html
NE1_50M_SR_W/tilemapresource.xml
```

Open the openlayers.html file in a web browser to see the results.[43]

[43] The default map loads a Google Maps layer, it will complain that you do not have an appropriate API key setup in the file, ignore it and switch to the OpenStreetMap layer in the right hand layer listing.

The resulting map should show your nicely coloured world map image from the Natural Earth dataset. The TMS Overlay option will show in the layer listing, so you can toggle it on/off to see that it truly is loading. Figure 9.1, on the next page shows the result of our gdal2tiles command.

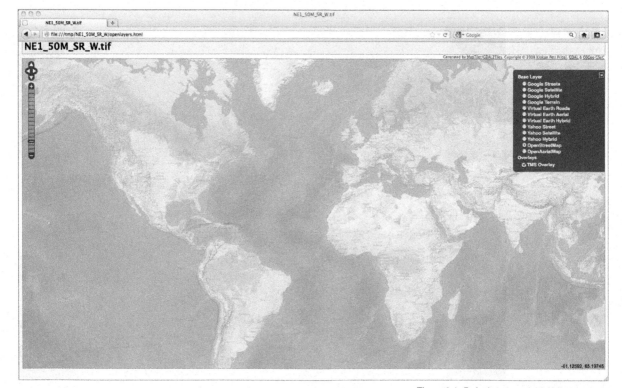

Figure 9.1: Default output of gdal2tiles process

Output KML for Google Earth

Google Earth can use files in a TMS structure and gdal2tiles has
a built-in facility for generating the KML file in the needed format.
This can be selected using the -k *force KML* option:

```
gdal2tiles.py -k -p geodetic NE1_50M_SR_W.tif
```

The result is called doc.kml and is found in the main output folder.
Open it in Google Earth and enjoy the results (Figure 9.2, on the
following page).

Viewing Non-Georeferenced Imagery

To use a non-georeferenced image, the -p raster profile must be
used. This creates a multi-resolution hierarchy of tiles just as before.

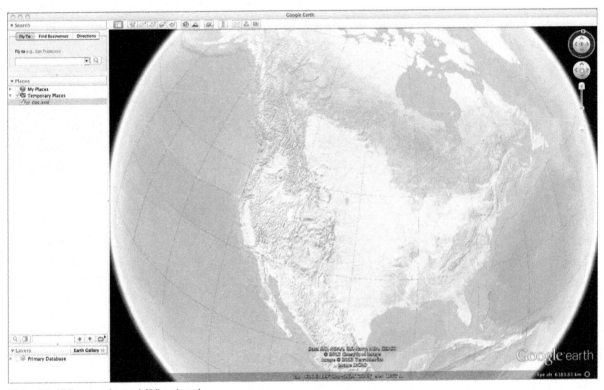

Figure 9.2: KML output from gdal2tiles viewed
in Google Earth

For example, here is an 89MB JPEG of Mona Lisa[44] (7479 x 11146
px):

44 "Mona Lisa, by Leonardo da Vinci, from
C2RMF retouched". Licensed under Public domain via Wikimedia Commons.

```
gdal2tiles.py -p raster mona_lisa.jpg
```

Open it in the openlayers.html viewer (Figure 9.3, on the next
page) and you have an easy, lightweight, image viewer that is so
much smarter than loading it full resolution in the browser.

Figure 9.3: Mona Lisa as a non-georeferenced
raster in the OpenLayers web viewer

10

MapServer Raster Tileindex - gdaltindex

MapServer[45] is a web mapping server application. It can present multiple rasters as a unified layer through its tileindex facility. A tile index is a shapefile with rectangles representing each image extent, and some attribute data pointing to the raster location on disk.

[45] http://mapserver.org

There are various options available; see gdaltindex on page 131 for details. The output specified is the name of the shapefile that will be created. The second parameter is a list of raster files. The command can be run multiple times to sequentially add more index rectangles to the file:

```
gdaltindex images.shp NE1_50M_SR_W/NE1_50M_SR_W.tif
```

This is a simple, one raster example. Here is one that would catalogue multiple files in a folder:

```
gdaltindex images.shp /NE1_50M_SR_W/*.tif
```

Check the output using ogrinfo to understand what it did:

```
ogrinfo images.shp -al
```

```
INFO: Open of `images.shp'
      using driver `ESRI Shapefile' successful.

Layer name: images
Geometry: Polygon
Feature Count: 1
Extent: (-180.000000, -90.000000) - (180.000000, 90.000000)
Layer SRS WKT:
GEOGCS["GCS_WGS_1984",
    DATUM["WGS_1984",
        SPHEROID["WGS_84",6378137,298.257223563]],
    PRIMEM["Greenwich",0],
    UNIT["Degree",0.0174532925199943295]]
location: String (255.0)
OGRFeature(images):0
location (String) = /NE1_50M_SR_W/NE1_50M_SR_W.tif
POLYGON ((-180.0 90.0,179.999 90.0,179.999 -89.999,
        -180.0 -89.999,-180.0 90.0))
```

A final example here will use a real set of two different images. First, create two sample images that will be used as input:

```
gdal_translate -projwin -124 60 -100 40 \
            NE1_50M_SR_W.tif ne1_part1.tif
gdal_translate -projwin 0 0 50 -65 \
            NE1_50M_SR_W.tif ne1_part2.tif
```

Then create the tile index for these two images:

```
gdaltindex ne1_both.shp ne1_part1.tif ne1_part2.tif
```

Figure 10.1, on the next page shows what this looks like when viewing this shapefile in QGIS. Here you can see the two outline rectangles, one for each input image as well as a simple background map to show how they are geographically placed. In this example, the plugin called Tile Index Viewer was enabled in QGIS to show both the index boundaries as well as a preview image within them.

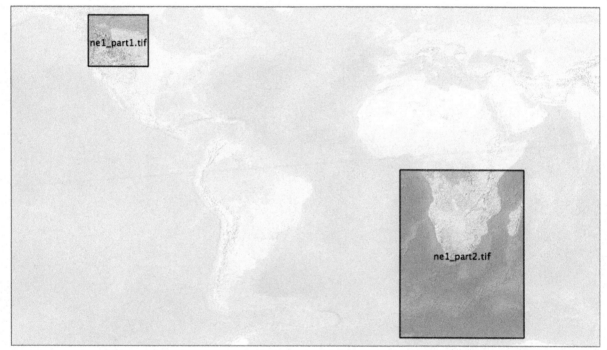

Figure 10.1: gdaltindex tile map example

11

MapServer Vector Tileindex - ogrtindex

The MapServer[46] web mapping platform has the ability to load a single OGR dataset that points to many different OGR layers and seamlessly present them as a single layer.

[46] http://mapserver.org

The `ogrtindex` utility is used to efficiently create the catalogue required to implement vector tiling. If the output file already exists, `ogrtindex` will append entries to it. All input layers must have the same number and type of columns/fields in order to be added to the index—this is required because MapServer will present it as a single layer.

In this example, the folder of Natural Earth datasets is used and each layer will be added to the index file; but first we will create some subsets that can be used as input for our example. Then we join it all together using `ogrtindex`:

```
ogr2ogr canada.shp 110m_admin_0_countries.shp -where 'NAME="Canada"'
ogr2ogr brazil.shp 110m_admin_0_countries.shp -where 'NAME="Brazil"'
ogr2ogr france.shp 110m_admin_0_countries.shp -where 'NAME="France"'

ogrtindex countries.shp canada.shp brazil.shp france.shp
```

Checking the dataset with `ogrinfo` shows that the three input features are all recorded as rows:

```
ogrinfo countries.shp -al -so

INFO: Open of `countries.shp'
      using driver `ESRI Shapefile' successful.

Layer name: countries
Geometry: Polygon
Feature Count: 3
Extent: (-140.997780, -33.768378) - (9.560016, 83.233240)
Layer SRS WKT:
GEOGCS["GCS_WGS_1984",
    DATUM["WGS_1984",
        SPHEROID["WGS_84",6378137.0,298.257223563]],
    PRIMEM["Greenwich",0.0],
    UNIT["Degree",0.017453292519943295]]
LOCATION: String (200.0)
```

Viewing this shapefile in a desktop (non-MapServer) application such as QGIS will show the bounding boxes of the input datasets (Figure 11.1, on the facing page).[47]

[47] The bounding box for France appears to include the geographic extent of French Guiana as well as the extent of the European country boundary.

This kind of tileindex is useful for general cataloguing of spatial data, but is normally only used by MapServer applications. For a general purpose virtual index option see the VRT format that allows you to catalog using an XML file and present it seamlessly to any application reading OGR datasets.

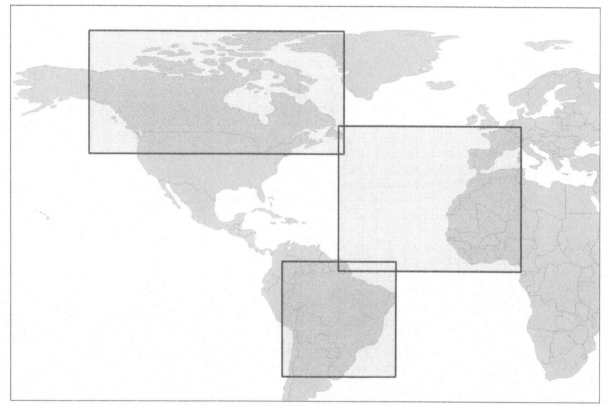

Figure 11.1: Bounding boxes stored in a MapServer tileindex shapefile

12

Virtual Raster Format - gdalbuildvrt

Contents

The Virtual Raster Format (VRT) file is an XML format file used to describe various raster datasets and have them viewed as a single entity by GDAL supported applications.[48] This operates similar to the output of gdaltindex but is more broadly usable than just in MapServer.

[48] There is also a **vector** VRT format - both are called VRT but catalogue/index differently.

Create a VRT from a folder of Rasters

In order to show how this command works, first we create two extracted images from a source file:

```
gdal_translate -projwin -124 60 -100 40 \
            NE1_50M_SR_W.tif ne1_part1.tif


Input file size is 10800, 5400
Computed -srcwin 1680 900 720 600 from projected window.
0...10...20...30...40...50...60...70...80...90...100 - done.

gdal_translate -projwin 0 0 50 -65 \
            NE1_50M_SR_W.tif ne1_part2.tif
```

```
Input file size is 10800, 5400
Computed -srcwin 5400 2700 1500 1950 from projected window.
```

The result are two separate image files. Next, use the gdalbuildvrt command to index/reference both files. A -vrtnodata option is specified so that blank spaces between the index rasters is filled with, in this case, transparency. In this example cells with the value 255 (e.g. in a greyscale image, this may be white) become transparent:

```
gdalbuildvrt -vrtnodata 255 ne1_parts.vrt \
            ne1_part1.tif ne1_part2.tif
```

This produces the ne1_parts.vrt file which can be read as an image file by GDAL command line utilities or applications that are built on GDAL libraries. When loaded into an application such as MapServer or QGIS, the rasters appear as a single layer, even though they are actually two separate files (see Figure 12.1, on the next page).

Using the -separate option you can also bring together three separate images and place each one in a different R, G, or B colour channel, thereby displaying a colour composite without having to merge the files into one.

With some of the most recent improvements with this command, you can also specify which band to use from each file. For example, using the SPOT Satellite Imagery from the Sample Data section, the multispectral IMAGERY.TIF file could be turned into a VRT file combining different bands into RGB output.

There are many more options available. For example, you can manually define the georeferenced extent of the VRT file using -te, as well as settting each input file as a separate band using the -separate option. See the gdalbuildvrt command reference on page 135 for a complete list.

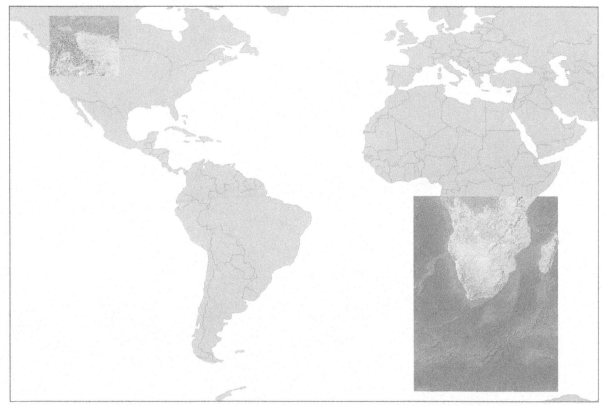

Figure 12.1: VRT file with two images virtually joined

13

Virtual Vector Format - ogr2vrt

Contents

Tips

- This is a Python script, and will only work if GDAL was built with Python support.
- This script is **not** included in most distributions but is an optional download from GDAL source code repository. Be sure to download the one that matches the version of GDAL you are using.[49]
- There is also a **raster** VRT format - both are called VRT but catalogue/index differently.

As described in the section on OGR Virtual Format on page 295:

[49] ogr2vrt.py script
latest: `http://loc8.cc/ogr2vrt`
[v1.9+]: `http://loc8.cc/ogr2vrt-1.9`

OGR Virtual Format is a driver that transforms features read from other drivers based on criteria specified in an XML control file.

For example, multiple files can be viewed as a single entity or (unioned) virtually or tables from ODBC connections can be transformed into spatial features, and more.

This operates similar to the output of `ogrtindex` but is more broadly usable than in just MapServer.

Aliasing a Vector file

There are many reasons you may want to create an alias for some of your data. In this example, the source vector file has an onerously long file name. We can shorten this using a VRT created by `ogr2vrt.py`.

The source file is:

```
ne/10m_cultural/ne_10m_admin_0_boundary_lines_disputed_areas.shp
```

Instead we want a file located at:

```
./disputed.vrt
```

To create this file, run the command (lines shortened for readability):

```
python ogr2vrt.py -relative \
  ne/10m_cultural/ne_10m_admin...disputed_areas.shp \
  disputed.vrt
```

Note that we use the `-relative` argument so that path names are stored as relative pointers from the VRT to the data files. This is optional depending on whether you have the data files in the same folder as the VRT or not.

If we open the VRT in QGIS, you will see the layer still has the original (long) layer name but is easily loaded via the shortened alias VRT file.

To change the layer name, simply edit the name property in the VRT file. For example, change:

```
<OGRVRTLayer name="ne_10m_admin...disputed_areas">
```

To something more readable:

```
<OGRVRTLayer name="ne_disputed">
```

Aliasing a folder of Vector files

The above example was a simple alias for a single layer, but the VRT file can serve as a more comprehensive vector datasource, containing a set of many layers. In this case you can use the ogr2vrt.py command to add each file in a folder, into the VRT file list. Each file then becomes a virtual layer in the output VRT XML:

```
python ogr2vrt.py -relative ne/10m_cultural 10m_cultural_all.vrt
```

If you load the resulting file into a GDAL/OGR supported application it finds all these layers and you can interact with them as you would normally.

In QGIS, for example, you still just select Layer -> Add Vector Layer -> File Browse and find the single VRT file, but then QGIS will prompt you to select which layers from the VRT you want to add to the map.

Aliasing a database connection

Just as above, a VRT file can be an alias to more than just files. In this case, you can connect to any OGR-enabled database and produce a VRT using ogr2vrt.py.

For example, you could refer to a PostGIS datasource and several layers, which would all be dumped into the resulting VRT:

```
python ogr2vrt.py PG:"dbname=ne user=x password=y" \
                  output.vrt ne.towns ne.rivers
```

Adding the output.vrt to QGIS will give you the choice of adding one of the two layers. You can modify this VRT to also be a union

VRT by simply adding a couple tags, see following sections for examples.

Aliasing a CSV file as a spatial layer

One of the most common uses of Vector VRT files is to act as a sort of connection point to non-spatial data sources that may have fields that include spatial data. For example, a CSV file with latitude and longitudes fields. CSV is not a spatial data file format, but can be made to act as one via VRT access.[50]

Naturally it would probably improve performance to convert these types of data sources into another format, but in cases where this is not possible, it's a quick way of moving forward.

[50] Note that some CSV formats can be read as spatial data files, for example, the Geonames format used in our sample data files is automatically recognised by OGR.

Here is a simple `sample.csv` file, using some basic data from Geonames Canada dataset:

```
id,name,name2,lat,long
4030308,Swiftsure Bank,48.55321,-125.02235
5881639,100 Mile House51.64982,-121.28594
5881640,101 Mile Lake51.6675,-121.29361
5881641,101 Ponds47.811,-53.97733
```

At this point you could hand-craft a VRT XML file, but `ogr2vrt.py` gives you a quicker headstart:

```
python ogr2vrt.py sample.csv sample.vrt
```

If you run `ogrinfo` on `sample.vrt` you will see that it has no geometry defined. To fix this we add two things - first, change the `GeometryType` element to `wkbPoint`. Second, add a `GeometryField` definition that references the lat/long fields as the source for building point geometries. See lines 6-8 below:

```
1    <OGRVRTDataSource>
2      <OGRVRTLayer name="sample">
3        <SrcDataSource relativeToVRT="0" shared="1">
4          sample.csv </SrcDataSource>
5        <SrcLayer>sample</SrcLayer>
```

```
6          <GeometryType>wkbPoint</GeometryType>
7          <GeometryField encoding="PointFromColumns"
8                          x="long" y="lat"/>
9          <Field name="id" type="String" src="id"/>
10         <Field name="name" type="String" src="name"/>
11         <Field name="lat" type="String" src="lat"/>
12         <Field name="long" type="String" src="long"/>
13      </OGRVRTLayer>
14   </OGRVRTDataSource>
```

Running `ogrinfo` on the VRT, you can see the point geometry is now present. The VRT file can be used (alongside the CSV) as an input for QGIS or other GDAL-enabled applications:

```
ogrinfo sample.vrt -al

Layer name: sample
Geometry: Point
Feature Count: 4
Extent: (-125.022350, -121.293610) - (0.000000, 48.553210)
...
OGRFeature(sample):1
  id (String) = 4030308
  name (String) = Swiftsure Bank
  lat (String) = 48.55321
  long (String) = -125.02235
  POINT (-125.02235 48.55321)
```

Create a Union VRT from a folder of Vector files

The real power of VRT files comes into play when you want create virtual representations of features as well. In this case, you can virtually tile together many individual layers as one. At the present time you cannot do this with a single command line but it only takes adding two simple lines to the VRT XML file to make it start working.

Here we want to create a virtual vector layer from all the files containing lines in the ne/10m_cultural folder. First, to keep it simple, create a folder and copy in only the files we are interested in:

```
mkdir ne/all_lines
cp ne/10m_cultural/*lines* ne/all_lines
```

Then we can create our VRT file as shown in the previous example:

```
python ogr2vrt.py -relative ne/all_lines all_lines.vrt
```

If added to QGIS at this point, it will merely present a list of four layers to select to load. This is not what we want.

Next we edit the all_lines.vrt file and add a set of *OGRVRTUnion-Layer* tags that tell GDAL/OGR the contents are to be presented as a unioned layer with a given name (i.e. "UnionedLines"). The added tag is the second one below, with the closing tag second from the end:

```
<OGRVRTDataSource>
 <OGRVRTUnionLayer name="UnionedLines">
  <OGRVRTLayer name="ne_10m_admin...disputed_areas">
   <SrcDataSource relativeToVRT="1" shared="1">

   ...
   <Field name="note" type="String" src="note" width="200"/>
  </OGRVRTLayer>
 </OGRVRTUnionLayer>
</OGRVRTDataSource>
```

Now loading it into QGIS automatically loads it as a single layer, but behind the scenes, it is a virtual representation of four layers.

On the map in Figure 13.1, on the facing page the unionedLines layer is drawn on top using red lines, whereas all the source files (that I manually loaded) are shown with a light shading. This shows that the new virtual layer covers all the source layer features.

Catalogue layers with varying geometry types

In our all_lines.vrt example earlier, we manually copied out a set of linestring layer files before cataloguing them. If you had simply catalogued the entire source folder, it would still work... sort of.

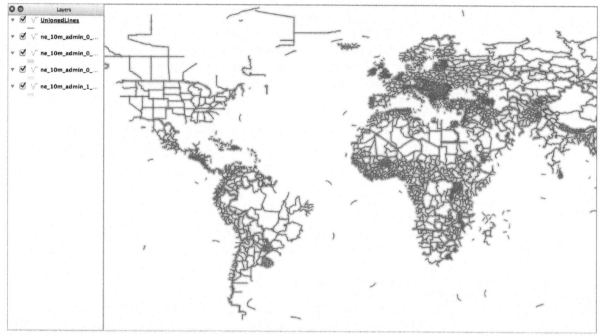

Figure 13.1: Unioned OGR VRT layers - source layers beneath final resulting merged layer

For example, if we had run:

```
python ogr2vrt.py  -relative ne/10m_cultural ne_10m_cult.vrt
```

It gives us a nice long VRT that is over 400 lines long. Some of the layers in there are linestring, polygon and point. So simply applying the OGRVRTUnionLayer tag won't really show all the layers in the virtual results.

Of course, if you sort the file and insert multiple OGRVRTUnionLayer elements then you could have a virtual layer for each geometry type. But there is one other way to quickly show one type of another.

What ends up happening is that apps, like QGIS, will likely treat all layers as having the geometry type of the first layer. To fix this, add a GeometryType element after the OGRVRTUnionLayer element when you add it. (Yes, you can ignore the geometry type elements that are in each subsequent layer):

```
<OGRVRTDataSource>
<OGRVRTUnionLayer name="ne_10m_cult">
<GeometryType>wkbPolygon</GeometryType>
<OGRVRTLayer name="ne_10m_admin...disputed_areas">
 <SrcDataSource relativeToVRT="1" shared="1">

 ...
```

The result will be that all the virtual sub-layers of that type will be displayed. This can be verified by running `ogrinfo` against the VRT to see what it reports its type as:

```
$ ogrinfo ne_10m_cult.vrt
INFO: Open of `ne_10m_cult.vrt'
      using driver `VRT' successful.
1: ne_10m_cult (Polygon)
```

Further Reading

For further options regarding VRT files see the more comprehensive reference on page 295 or see the CSV specific documentation on page 289.

14

Raster Mosaics - gdal_merge

> **Tip**
>
> This is a Python script, and will only work if GDAL was built with Python support.

The gdal_merge command mosaics multiple rasters into a single new image. Two issues to keep in mind when doing mosaics: pixel sizes can be manipulated and the "background" colour of the new image may not default as desired, so it can be set as well.

Create a Mosaic of Two Rasters

This example uses two raster subsets created in an earlier chapter. The first option, -init specifies the output colour to use as the background for the new image. Any area in the input images where there is no raster data will be given this colour. In this case we use a value that provides a medium grey tone when rendered as a greyscale image. The second option, -o merely specifies the output filename to create:

```
gdal_merge.py -init "100" -o ne_merged.tif \
            ne1_part1.tif ne1_part2.tif
```

The result is a single image with both source images included as shown in Figure 14.1.

Figure 14.1: Merged - Two raster files into one

Part III

GDAL Raster Utilities

Table of Contents

1

Application Groupings

Reporting

gdalinfo:
Report information about a file

gdal-config:
Get options required to build software using GDAL

gdallocationinfo:
Query raster at a location

Translate & Transform

gdal_translate:
Copy a raster file, with control of output format

gdal_rasterize:
Rasterize vectors into raster file

gdaltransform:
Transform coordinates

gdalmove.py:
Transform georeferencing of raster file in place (Python)

Adjust & Optimise

gdaladdo:
Add overviews to a file

gdalwarp:
Warp an image into a new coordinate system

rgb2pct.py:
Convert a 24bit RGB image to 8bit paletted

pct2rgb.py:
Convert an 8bit paletted image to 24bit RGB

nearblack:
Convert nearly black/white borders to exact value

gdal_sieve.py:
Raster Sieve filter (Python)

Generate Data

gdaltindex:
Build a MapServer raster tileindex

gdalbuildvrt:
Build a VRT from a list of datasets

gdal_merge:
Build a quick mosaic from a set of images

gdal2tiles:
Create a TMS tile structure, KML and simple web viewer

gdal_retile.py:
Retiles a set of tiles and/or build tiled pyramid levels (Python)

gdal_grid:
Create raster from the scattered data

gdal_proximity.py:
Compute a raster proximity map (Python)

gdal_polygonize.py:
Generate polygons from raster (Python)

gdal_fillnodata.py:
Interpolate in nodata regions (Python)

Elevation Models

gdal_contour:
> Contours from DEM

gdaldem:
> Tools to analyze and visualize DEMs

Creating New Files

Accessing an existing file to read is generally quite simple. Just indicate the name of the file or dataset on the command line. However, creating a new file is more complicated. It may be necessary to indicate the format to create, various creation options affecting how it will be created, and perhaps a coordinate system to be assigned. Many of these options are handled similarly by different GDAL utilities, and are introduced here.

General Command Line Switches

All GDAL command line utility programs support the following "general" options.

--version
> Report the version of GDAL and exit.

–formats
> List all raster formats supported by this GDAL build (read-only and read-write) and exit. The format support is indicated as follows: 'ro' is read-only driver; 'rw' is read or write (i.e. supports CreateCopy); 'rw+' is read, write and update (i.e. supports Create). A 'v' is appended for formats supporting virtual IO (/vsimem, /vsigzip, /vsizip, etc). Note: The valid formats for the output of gdalwarp are formats that support the Create() method (marked as rw+), not just the CreateCopy() method.

--format format
> List detailed information about a single format driver. The format should be the short name reported in the **--formats** list, such as GTiff.

--optfile file
> Read the named file and substitute the contents into the command line options list. Lines beginning with # will be ignored. Multi-word arguments may be kept together with double quotes.

--config key value
> Sets the named configuration keyword[51] to the given value, as opposed to setting them as environment variables. Some common configuration keywords are GDAL_CACHEMAX (memory used internally for caching in megabytes) and GDAL_DATA (path of the GDAL data directory). Individual drivers may be influenced by other configuration options.

--debug value
> Control what debugging messages are emitted. A value of ON will enable all debug messages. A value of OFF will disable all debug messages. Another value will filter the responses and show only debug messages containing that string in the debug prefix code. Some drivers will return specific debug info if you provide their name, e.g. NETCDF, but most debug code falls under the generic GDAL prefix.

--help-general
> Gives a brief usage message for the generic GDAL command line options and exit.

[51] http://trac.osgeo.org/gdal/wiki/ConfigOptions

2

gdalinfo

LISTS INFORMATION ABOUT A RASTER DATASET

Syntax

```
gdalinfo    [--help-general] [-mm] [-stats] [-approx_stats]
            [-hist] [-nogcp] [-nomd] [-norat] [-noct]
            [-checksum] [-mdd domain]* [-nofl]
            [-sd subdataset] [-proj4] datasetname
```

The gdalinfo program lists various information about a GDAL supported raster dataset.

-*mm*:

   Force computation of the actual min/max values for each band in the dataset.

-*stats*:

   Read and display image statistics. Force computation if no statistics are stored in an image.

-*approx_stats*:

   Read and display image statistics. Force computation if no statistics are stored in an image. However, they may be computed based on overviews or a subset of all tiles. Useful if you are in a hurry and don't want precise stats.

-hist:

    Report histogram information for all bands.

-nogcp:

    Suppress ground control points list printing. It may be useful for datasets with huge amount of GCPs, such as L1B AVHRR or HDF4 MODIS which contain thousands of ones.

-nomd:

    Suppress metadata printing. Some datasets may contain a lot of metadata strings.

-norat:

    Suppress printing of raster attribute table.

-noct:

    Suppress printing of color table.

-checksum:

    Force computation of the checksum for each band in the dataset.

-mdd domain:

    Report metadata for the specified domain

-nofl: [v1.9+]

    Only display the first file of the file list.

-sd subdataset: [v1.9+]

    If the input dataset contains several subdatasets read and display a subdataset with specified number (starting from 1). This is an alternative of giving the full subdataset name.

-proj4: [v1.9+]

    Report a PROJ.4 string corresponding to the file's coordinate system.

Results

The gdalinfo command will report all of the following (if known):

Format

- The format driver used to access the file

Size

- Raster size (in pixels and lines)

Coordinate System

- The coordinate system for the file (in OGC[52] WKT[53])
- The geotransform associated with the file (rotational coefficients are currently not reported)
- Corner coordinates in georeferenced, and if possible lat/long based on the full geotransform (but not GCPs)
- Ground control points (GCPs)

Metadata

- File wide (including subdatasets) metadata.

Band Information

- Band data types
- Band color interpretations
- Band block size
- Band descriptions
- Band min/max values (internally known and possibly computed)
- Band checksum (if computation asked)
- Band NODATA value
- Band overview resolutions available
- Band unit type (i.e.. "meters" or "feet" for elevation bands)
- Band pseudo-color tables

[52] Open Geo. Consortium: http://loc8.cc/ogc

[53] Well-Known Text format: http://loc8.cc/wkt

Example

Report information on the raster file utm.tif using gdalinfo:

```
gdalinfo utm.tif

Driver: GTiff/GeoTIFF
Size is 512, 512
Coordinate System is:
PROJCS["NAD27 / UTM zone 11N",
  GEOGCS["NAD27",
    DATUM["North_American_Datum_1927",
      SPHEROID["Clarke 1866",6378206.4,294.978698]],
    PRIMEM["Greenwich",0],
    UNIT["degree",0.0174532925199433]],
    PROJECTION["Transverse_Mercator"],
    PARAMETER["latitude_of_origin",0],
    PARAMETER["central_meridian",-117],
    PARAMETER["scale_factor",0.9996],
    PARAMETER["false_easting",500000],
    PARAMETER["false_northing",0],
    UNIT["metre",1]]
Origin = (440720.000000,3751320.000000)
Pixel Size = (60.000000,-60.000000)
Corner Coordinates:
Upper Left  (  440720, 3751320) (117d38'28.21"W, 33d54'8.47"N)
Lower Left  (  440720, 3720600) (117d38'20.79"W, 33d37'31.04"N)
Upper Right (  471440, 3751320) (117d18'32.07"W, 33d54'13.08"N)
Lower Right (  471440, 3720600) (117d18'28.50"W, 33d37'35.61"N)
Center      (  456080, 3735960) (117d28'27.39"W, 33d45'52.46"N)
Band 1 Block=512x16 Type=Byte, ColorInterp=Gray
```

3

gdal_translate

CONVERTS RASTER DATA BETWEEN DIFFERENT FORMATS

Syntax

```
gdal_translate [--help-general] [-ot type] [-strict]
      [-of format] [-b band] [-mask band]
      [-expand {gray|rgb|rgba}]
      [-outsize xsize[%] ysize[%]]
      [-unscale]
      [-scale [src_min src_max [dst_min dst_max]]]
      [-srcwin xoff yoff xsize ysize]
      [-projwin ulx uly lrx lry]
      [-epo] [-eco] [-a_srs srs_def]
      [-a_ullr ulx uly lrx lry]
      [-a_nodata value]
      [-gcp pixel line easting northing [elevation]]*
      [-mo "META-TAG=VALUE"]* [-q] [-sds]
      [-co "NAME=VALUE"]* [-stats]
      src_dataset dst_dataset
```

The gdal_translate utility can be used to convert raster data between
different formats, potentially performing some operations like subsetting, resampling, and rescaling pixels in the process.

-ot *type:*
> Select the data type for the output bands: Byte, Int16, UInt16, UInt32 Int32, Float32, Float64, CInt16, CInt32, CFloat32, CFloat64.

-strict:
> Don't be forgiving of mismatches and lost data when translating to the output format.

-of *format:*
> Specify the output format. The default is GeoTIFF (GTiff). Use the short format name that is listed when the command is run with no parameters or with the --formats flag.[54]

[54] See the Raster Data Formats chapter on page 331 for a listing of formats.

-b *band:*
> Select an input band *band* for output. Bands are numbered starting from 1. Multiple -b switches may be used to select a set of input bands to write to the output file, or to reorder bands.
>
> **[v1.8+]** - *band* can also be set to mask,1 (or just mask) to mean the mask band of the 1st band of the input dataset.

-mask *band:* *[v1.8+]*
> Select an input band *band* to create output dataset mask band. Bands are numbered starting from 1.
>
> *band* can be set to none to avoid copying the global mask of the input dataset if it exists. Otherwise it is copied by default (auto), unless the mask is an alpha channel, or if it is explicitly used to be a regular band of the output dataset (-b mask).
>
> *band* can also be set to mask,1 (or just mask) to mean the mask band of the 1st band of the input dataset.

-expand gray | rgb | rgba: *[v1.6+]*
> To expose a dataset with 1 band with a color table as a dataset with 3 (RGB) or 4 (RGBA) bands. Useful for output drivers such as JPEG, JPEG2000, MrSID, ECW that don't support color indexed datasets. The *gray* value (**[v1.7+]**) enables to expand a dataset with a color table that only contains gray levels to a gray indexed dataset.

-outsize *xsize[%] ysize[%]:*
> Set the size of the output file. Outsize is in pixels and lines unless

'%' is attached in which case it is set as a fraction of the input image size.

-scale [src_min src_max [dst_min dst_max]]:
Rescale the input pixels values from the range *src_min* to *src_max* to the range *dst_min* to *dst_max*. If omitted the output range is 0 to 255. If omitted the input range is automatically computed from the source data.

-unscale:
Apply the scale/offset metadata for the bands to convert scaled values to unscaled values. It is also often necessary to reset the output datatype with the -ot switch.

-srcwin xoff yoff xsize ysize:
Selects a subwindow from the source image for copying based on pixel/line location.

-projwin ulx uly lrx lry:
Selects a subwindow from the source image for copying (like -**srcwin**) but with the corners given in georeferenced coordinates.

-epo: [v1.10+]
Error when Partially Outside - If this option is set, -srcwin or -projwin values that falls partially outside the source raster extent will be considered as an error. The default behaviour starting with GDAL 1.10 is to accept such requests, when they were considered as an error before.

-eco: [v1.10+]
Error when Completely Outside - Same as -epo, except that the criterion for erroring out is when the request falls completely outside the source raster extent.

-a_srs srs_def:
Override the projection for the output file. The *srs_def* may be any of the usual GDAL/OGR forms: complete WKT, PROJ.4, EPSG:n or a file containing the WKT.

-a_ullr ulx uly lrx lry:
Assign/override the georeferenced bounds of the output file. This assigns georeferenced bounds to the output file, ignoring what would have been derived from the source file.

-a_nodata value:
> Assign a specified *nodata* value to output bands. Starting with GDAL 1.8.0, can be set to *none* to avoid setting a *nodata* value to the output file if one exists for the source file.

-mo "META-TAG=VALUE":
> Passes a metadata key and value to set on the output dataset if possible.

-co "NAME=VALUE":
> Passes a creation option to the output format driver. Multiple -co options may be listed. See format specific documentation for legal creation options for each format.

-gcp pixel line easting northing elevation:
> Add the indicated ground control point to the output dataset. This option may be provided multiple times to provide a set of GCPs.

-q:
> Suppress progress monitor and other non-error output.

-sds:
> Copy all subdatasets of this file to individual output files. Use with formats like HDF or OGDI that have subdatasets.

-stats: [v1.8+]
> Force (re)computation of statistics.

src_dataset:
> The source dataset name. It can be either file name, URL of data source or subdataset name for multi-dataset files.

dst_dataset:
> The destination file name.

Examples

Convert a TIFF image from strip to tiled[55] internal format (where data is stored in two dimensional tiles instead of one dimensional strips) with each tile being of equal size and compressed independently:

```
gdal_translate -of GTiff -co "TILED=YES" utm.tif utm_tiled.tif
```

[55] TIFF Tiles: http://loc8.cc/tiff_tiles

Convert a TIFF image and apply JPEG-compression to the new image, while *also* creating a mask band **[v1.8+]** in the image:

```
gdal_translate rgba.tif withmask.tif -b 1 -b 2 -b 3 -mask 4
  -co COMPRESS=JPEG --config GDAL_TIFF_INTERNAL_MASK YES
```

Convert a three band TIFF containing red, green, blue (RGB) forms into the RGBA form that includes an alpha mask layer **[v1.8+]**. Each band to be used is specified using the -b options and the mask layer is identified as well:

```
gdal_translate withmask.tif rgba.tif -b 1 -b 2 -b 3 -b mask
```

4

gdaladdo

BUILDS OR REBUILDS OVERVIEW IMAGES

Syntax

```
gdaladdo [-r {nearest,average,gauss,cubic,average_mp,average_magphase,mode}]
         [-ro] [-clean] [--help-general] filename levels
```

Description

The gdaladdo utility can be used to build or rebuild overview images for most supported file formats with one of several downsampling algorithms.

-r {nearest (default),average,gauss,cubic,average_mp,average_magphase,mode}:
Select a resampling algorithm.

-ro: [v1.6+]
Open the dataset in read-only mode, in order to generate external overview (for GeoTIFF especially).

-clean: [v1.7+]
Remove all overviews.

filename:
The file to build overviews for (or whose overviews must be removed).

levels:

A list of integral overview levels to build. Ignored with
-clean option.

Resampling algorithms

mode: [v1.6+]
Selects the value which appears most often of all the
sampled points.

average_mp:
is unsuitable for use.

average_magphase:
averages complex data in mag/phase space.

nearest and average:
are applicable to normal image data.

nearest:
applies a nearest neighbour (simple sampling) re-
sampler.

average:
computes the average of all non-NODATA contribut-
ing pixels.

Cubic: resampling [v1.7+]
Applies a 4x4 approximate cubic convolution kernel.

Gauss: resampling [v1.6+] applies a
Gaussian kernel before computing the overview, which can
lead to better results than simple averaging in e.g case of
sharp edges with high contrast or noisy patterns. The ad-
vised level values should be 2, 4, 8, etc., so that a 3x3 resampling Gaussian kernel is selected.

gdaladdo will honour proper NODATA_VALUES tuples (special
dataset metadata) so that only a given RGB triplet (in case of a RGB
image) will be considered as the nodata value and not each value of
the triplet independently per band.

Selecting a level value like 2 causes an overview level that is 1/2 the resolution (in each dimension) of the base layer to be computed. If the file has existing overview levels at a level selected, those levels will be recomputed and rewritten in place.

Some format drivers do not support overviews at all. Many format drivers store overviews in a secondary file with the extension .ovr that is actually in TIFF format. By default, the GeoTIFF driver stores overviews internally to the file operated on (if it is writable), unless the -ro flag is specified.

Most drivers also support an alternate overview format using Erdas Imagine format. To trigger this use the USE_RRD=YES configuration option:

```
--config USE_RRD=YES
```

This will place the overviews in an associated .aux file suitable for direct use with Imagine or ArcGIS as well as applications using GDAL for raster support.

External Overviews in GeoTIFF format

External overviews created in TIFF format may be **compressed** using the COMPRESS_OVERVIEW configuration option. All compression methods, supported by the GeoTIFF driver, are available here. (e.g. COMPRESS_OVERVIEW DEFLATE).

The **photometric** interpretation can be set with:

```
--config PHOTOMETRIC_OVERVIEW {RGB,YCBCR,...}
```

and the **interleaving** with:

```
--config INTERLEAVE_OVERVIEW {PIXEL\|BAND}
```

For JPEG compressed external overviews, the JPEG **quality** can be set [v1.7+] with:

```
--config JPEG_QUALITY_OVERVIEW value
```

For LZW or DEFLATE compressed external overviews, the **predictor** value can be set [**v1.8+**] with:

```
--config PREDICTOR_OVERVIEW 1|2|3
```

To produce the **smallest possible** JPEG-In-TIFF overviews, you should use:

```
--config COMPRESS_OVERVIEW JPEG
--config PHOTOMETRIC_OVERVIEW YCBCR
--config INTERLEAVE_OVERVIEW PIXEL
```

External overviews can be created in the **BigTIFF** format [**v1.7+**] by using the BIGTIFF_OVERVIEW configuration option:

```
--config BIGTIFF_OVERVIEW {IF_NEEDED|IF_SAFER|YES|NO}
```

The default value is IF_NEEDED. The behaviour of this option is exactly the same as the BIGTIFF creation option documented in the GeoTIFF driver documentation.

- YES forces BigTIFF.
- NO forces classic TIFF.
- IF_NEEDED will only create a BigTIFF if it is clearly needed (uncompressed, and overviews larger than 4GB).
- IF_SAFER will create BigTIFF if the resulting file *might* exceed 4GB.

See the documentation of the GeoTIFF[56] driver for further explanations on all those options.

[56] http://loc8.cc/gdal_gtiff

Examples

Create overviews, embedded in the supplied TIFF file:

```
gdaladdo -r average abc.tif 2 4 8 16
```

Create an external compressed GeoTIFF overview file from the ERDAS .IMG file:

```
gdaladdo -ro --config COMPRESS_OVERVIEW DEFLATE \
        erdas.img 2 4 8 16
```

Create an external JPEG-compressed GeoTIFF overview file from a 3-band RGB dataset (if the dataset is a writable GeoTIFF, you also need to add the -ro option to force the generation of external overview):

```
gdaladdo --config COMPRESS_OVERVIEW JPEG \
        --config PHOTOMETRIC_OVERVIEW YCBCR \
        --config INTERLEAVE_OVERVIEW PIXEL \
        rgb_dataset.ext 2 4 8 16
```

Create an Erdas Imagine format overviews for the indicated JPEG file:

```
gdaladdo --config USE_RRD YES airphoto.jpg 3 9 27 81
```

5

gdaltindex

Syntax

```
gdaltindex [-f format]
           [-tileindex field_name]
           [-write_absolute_path]
           [-skip_different_projection]
           [-t_srs target_srs]
           [-src_srs_name field_name]
           [-src_srs_format [AUTO|WKT|EPSG|PROJ]
           [-lyr_name name]
           index_file
           [gdal_file]*
```

Description

This program builds a shapefile with a record for each input raster file, an attribute containing the filename, and a polygon geometry outlining the raster. This output is suitable for use with MapServer[57] as a raster tileindex.

Simple rectangular polygons are generated in the same coordinate reference system as the rasters, or in target reference system if the

-t_srs option is used.

-f format: [v2.0+]
The OGR format of the output tile index file. Default is Esri Shapefile.

-tileindex field_name:
The output field name to hold the file path/location to the indexed rasters. The default tile index field name is location.

-write_absolute_path:
The absolute path to the raster files is stored in the tile index file. By default the raster filenames will be put in the file exactly as they are specified on the command line.

-skip_different_projection:
Only files with same projection as files already inserted in the tileindex will be inserted (unless -t_srs is specified). Default does not check projection and accepts all inputs.

-t_srs target_srs:
Geometries of input files will be transformed to the desired target coordinate reference system. Using this option generates files that are not compatible with MapServer < 6.4. Default creates simple rectangular polygons in the same coordinate reference system as the input rasters.

-src_srs_name field_name: [v2.0+]
The name of the field to store the SRS of each tile. This field name can be used as the value of the TILESRS keyword in MapServer >= 6.4.

-src_srs_format type: [v2.0+]
The format in which the SRS of each tile must be written. Types can be AUTO, WKT, EPSG, PROJ.

-lyr_name name:
Layer name to create/append to in the output tile index file.

EXAMPLE   133

index_file:

> The name of the output file to create/append to. The default shapefile will be created if it doesn't already exist, otherwise it will append to the existing file.

gdal_file:

> The input GDAL raster files, can be multiple files separated by spaces. Wildcards my also be used. Stores the file locations in the same style as specified here, unless -write_absolute_path option is also used.

Example

Create a tile index shapefile (doq_index.shp) with a record for every image that the utility found in the doq folder. Each record holds information that points to the location of the image and also a bounding rectangle shape showing the bounds of the image:

```
gdaltindex doq_index.shp doq/*.tif
```

The -t_srs option can also be used to transform all input raster files into a common output projection:

```
gdaltindex -t_srs EPSG:4326 -src_srs_name src_srs \
        tile_index_mixed_srs.shp *.tif
```

6

gdalbuildvrt

BUILDS A VRT FILE FROM A LIST OF RASTER DATASETS

Syntax

```
gdalbuildvrt [-tileindex field_name]
             [-resolution {highest|lowest|average|user}]
             [-tr xres yres] [-tap] [-separate] [-b band]
             [-allow_projection_difference] [-q]
             [-te xmin ymin xmax ymax] [-addalpha] [-hidenodata]
             [-srcnodata "value [value...]"]
             [-vrtnodata "value [value...]"]
             [-input_file_list my_list.txt] [-overwrite]
             output.vrt [gdalfile]*
```

Description

[58] VRT: http://loc8.cc/gdal_vrt

The VRT (Virtual Dataset) driver[58] is a format driver for GDAL that allows a virtual GDAL dataset to be composed from other GDAL datasets with repositioning, and algorithms potentially applied as well as various kinds of metadata altered or added. VRT descriptions of datasets can be saved in an XML format normally given the extension .vrt.

This program builds a VRT that is a mosaic of the list of input GDAL datasets.

The list of input GDAL datasets can be specified at the end of the command line, or put in a text file (one filename per line) for very long lists, or it can be a MapServer tileindex (see gdaltindex utility). In the latter case, all entries in the tile index will be added to the VRT.

With **-separate**, each file goes into a separate *stacked* band in the VRT band. Otherwise, the files are considered tiles of a larger mosaic and the VRT file has as many bands as one of the input files.

If one GDAL dataset is made of several subdatasets and has 0 raster bands, all the subdatasets will be added to the VRT rather than the dataset itself.

By default, gdalbuildvrt generally checks to assure that all files that will be put in the resulting VRT have similar characteristics: number of bands, projection, color interpretation, etc. If not, files that do not match the common characteristics will be skipped. The -separate option overrides the default behaviour.

If there is spatial overlap between files, care must be taken to specify the sequence in which they should be optimally presented in the VRT. Files that are "on top" of other files may occlude files that overlap "beneath" them as they are layered together in the VRT. gdalbuildvrt may try to adjust this automatically, but this behaviour should not be relied on.

-tileindex:
Use the specified value as the tile index field name. Default name: location.

-resolution {highest | lowest | average | user}:
In case the resolution of all input files is not the same, the -resolution flag enables the user to control the way the output resolution is computed.

average: is the default.

highest: picks the smallest values of pixel dimensions (highest resolution) within the set of source rasters.

lowest: picks the largest values of pixel dimensions (lowest resolution) within the set of source rasters.

average: computes an average of pixel dimensions within the set of source rasters.

user: **[v1.7+]** user-defined - must be used in combination with the -tr option to specify the target resolution.

-tr xres yres: [v1.7+]

Set target resolution. The values must be expressed in georeferenced units. Both must be positive values. Specifying those values is of course incompatible with highest | lowest | average values for -resolution option.

-tap: [v1.8+]

Target Aligned Pixels - align the coordinates of the extent of the output file to the values of the -tr, such that the aligned extent includes the minimum extent.

-te xmin ymin xmax ymax: [v1.7+]

Set georeferenced extents of VRT file. The values must be expressed in georeferenced units. If not specified, the extent of the VRT is the minimum bounding box of the set of source rasters.

-addalpha: [v1.7+]

Adds an alpha mask band to the VRT when the source raster have none. Mainly useful for RGB sources (or grey-level sources). The alpha band is filled on-the-fly with the value 0 in areas without any source raster, and with value 255 in areas with source raster. The effect is that a RGBA viewer will render the areas without source rasters as transparent and areas with source rasters as opaque. **This option is not compatible with -separate.**

-hidenodata: [v1.7+]

Even if any band contains NODATA value, giving this option makes the VRT band not report the NODATA. Useful when you want to control the background color of the dataset. By using along with the -addalpha option, you can prepare a dataset which doesn't report nodata value but is transparent in areas with no data.

-srcnodata value [value...]: [v1.7+]

Set nodata values for input bands (different values can be supplied for each band). If more than one value is supplied all values should be quoted to keep them together as a single operating system argument. If the option is not specified, the intrinsic nodata settings on the source datasets will be used (if they exist). The value set by this option is written in the NODATA element of each ComplexSource element. Use a value of None to ignore intrinsic nodata settings on the source datasets.

-vrtnodata value [value...]: [v1.7+]

Set nodata values at the VRT band level (different values can be supplied for each band). If more than one value is supplied all values should be quoted to keep them together as a single operating system argument. If the option is not specified, intrinsic nodata settings on the first dataset will be used (if they exist). The value set by this option is written in the NoDataValue element of each VRTRasterBand element. Use a value of None to ignore intrinsic nodata settings on the source datasets.

-separate: [v1.7+]

Place each input file into a separate *stacked* band. Only the first band of each dataset will be placed into a new band. Contrary to the default mode, it is not required that all bands have the same datatype. This option is not compatible with -addalpha.

-b band: [v1.10+]

Select an input band to be processed. Bands are numbered from 1. If input bands not set all bands will be added to VRT.

-allow_projection_difference: [v1.7+]

Ignore the projections of the input datasets.

-input_file_list mylist.txt:

Specify a text file with input GDAL file names on each line.

-q: [v1.7+]

Disable the progress bar on the console.

-overwrite:

Overwrite the VRT if it already exists.

output.vrt: Output file name to create.

gdalfile: Input file names to include in the VRT. Not required if `-input_file_list` is specified.

Examples

Create a VRT file that catalogs all the `.tif` files in a folder:

```
gdalbuildvrt doq_index.vrt doq/*.tif
```

Create a VRT file that catalogs a list of raster files that are provided in a text file. One input filename is provided on each line of the text file:

```
gdalbuildvrt -input_file_list my_list.txt doq_index.vrt
```

Create a VRT that represents an RGB image, using three separate files, each representing one of the R, G, or B bands:

```
gdalbuildvrt -separate rgb.vrt red.tif green.tif blue.tif
```

Create a VRT file that catalogs all the `.tif` files in a folder, ignoring (hiding) existing NODATA values and replacing them with a specified NODATA value in the result:

```
gdalbuildvrt -hidenodata -vrtnodata "0 0 255" \
             index.vrt doq/*.tif
```

7

gdal_contour

Syntax

```
Usage: gdal_contour [-b <band>] [-a <attribute_name>]
                    [-3d] [-inodata]
                    [-snodata n] [-f <formatname>]
                    [-i <interval>]* [-off <offset>]
                    [-fl <level> <level>...]*
                    [-nln <outlayername>]
                    src_filename dst_filename
```

Description

This program generates a vector contour file from the input raster elevation model (DEM).

Starting at version 1.7, the contour line-strings will be oriented consistently. The high side will be on the right, i.e. a line string goes clockwise around a hill top.

The program requires input and output filenames as well one of -i *interval* or -fl *fixed levels* options to set what range of contours will be calculated.

-b band:
Specify the particular band to build the DEM from. Defaults to band 1.

-a name:
Name the attribute in which to put the elevation. If not provided no elevation attribute is attached.

-3d:
Force production of 3D vectors instead of the 2D default. Includes elevation at every vertex.

-inodata:
Ignore any nodata value implied in the dataset—treat all values as valid.

-snodata value:
Treat this input pixel value as nodata.

-f format:
Create output in a particular format, default is ESRI Shapefile.

-i interval:
Elevation interval between contours.

-off offset:
Relative offset, from zero, to which to interpret intervals.

-fl level [level]...:
Name one or more "fixed levels" to extract, separated by a space.

-nln outlayername:
Provide a name for the output vector layer. Defaults to *contour*.

src_filename:
Source raster filename.

dst_filename:
Destination vector filename.

Example

Create contours at 10 meter intervals (-i) from the DEM data in dem.tif and produce a shapefile named contour.shp with the contour elevations in the elev attribute (-a):

EXAMPLE   143

```
gdal_contour -a elev dem.tif contour.shp -i 10.0
```

Create contours at fixed elevation levels: 25, 50, and 100 metres, from DEM data in dem.tif and produce contour.shp:

```
gdal_contour -fl 25 50 100 dem.tif contour.shp
```

8

gdal_rasterize

BURNS VECTOR GEOMETRIES INTO A RASTER

Syntax

```
Usage: gdal_rasterize [-b band]* [-i] [-at]
       [-burn value]* | [-a attribute_name]
       [-3d] [-l layername]* [-where expression]
       [-sql select_statement] [-of format]
       [-a_srs srs_def] [-co "NAME=VALUE"]*
       [-a_nodata value] [-init value]*
       [-te xmin ymin xmax ymax] [-tr xres yres]
       [-tap] [-ts width height]
       [-ot type] [-q]
       src_datasource dst_filename
```

Description

This program burns vector geometries (points, lines and polygons) into the raster band(s) of a raster image. Vectors are read from OGR supported vector formats.

Note that the vector data must be in the same coordinate system as the raster data; on-the-fly reprojection is not provided.

Input OGR datasource and output GDAL filename parameters are required. As well as one of -l or -sql to specify the input layers to use.

The target GDAL file can be created by gdal_rasterize . One of -tr or -ts options must be used in that case. [v1.8+] Both options may not be used together.

-b *band:*
: The band(s) to burn values into. Multiple -b arguments may be used to burn into a list of bands. The default is to burn into band 1.

-i:
: Invert rasterization. Burn the fixed burn value, or the burn value associated with the first feature, into all parts of the image *not* inside the provided polygon.

-at:
: Enables the ALL_TOUCHED rasterization option so that all pixels touched by lines or polygons will be updated not just those on the line render path, or whose center point is within the polygon. Defaults to disabled for normal rendering rules.

-burn *value:*
: A fixed value to burn into a band for all objects. A list of -burn options can be supplied, one per band being written to.

-a *attribute_name:*
: Identifies an attribute field on the features to be used for a burn value. The value will be burned into all output bands.

-3d:
: Extract burn value from the "Z" values of the feature. These values are adjusted by the burn value given by -burn value or -a attribute_name if provided. As of now, only points and lines are drawn in 3D.

-l *layername:*
: Indicates the layer(s) from the datasource that will be used for input features. May be specified multiple times.

At least one layer name or a -sql option must be specified.

-where expression:

An optional SQL WHERE-style query expression to be applied to select features to burn in from the input layer(s).

-sql select_statement:

An SQL statement to be evaluated against the datasource to produce a virtual layer of features to be burned in.

At least `-sql` or one layer name `-l` option must be specified.

-of format: [v1.8+]

Select the output format. The default is GeoTIFF (GTiff). Use the short format name.[59]

-a_nodata value: [v1.8+]

Assign a specified nodata value to output bands.

-init value: [v1.8+]

Pre-initialize the output image bands with these values. However, it is not marked as the nodata value in the output file. If only one value is given, the same value is used in all the bands.

-a_srs srs_def: [v1.8+]

Override the projection for the output file. If not specified, the projection of the input vector file will be used if available.

If projections between input and output files are incompatible no attempt will be made to reproject features. The *srs_def* may be any of the usual GDAL/OGR forms, complete WKT, PROJ.4, EPSG:n or a file containing the WKT.

-co "NAME=VALUE": [v1.8+]

Passes a creation option to the output format driver. Multiple `-co` options may be listed. See format specific documentation for legal creation options for each format.

-te xmin ymin xmax ymax: [v1.8+]

Set georeferenced extents. The values must be expressed in georeferenced units. If not specified, the extent of the output file will be the extent of the vector layers.

-tr xres yres: [v1.8+]

Set target resolution. The values must be expressed in georeferenced units. Both must be positive values.

[59] See the Raster Data Formats chapter on page 331 for short format names.

Note that -tr cannot be used with -ts.

-tap: [v1.8+]
Target aligned pixels - align the coordinates of the extent of the output file to the values of the -tr, such that the aligned extent includes the minimum extent.

-ts width height: [v1.8+]
Set output file size in pixels and lines.

Note that -ts cannot be used with -tr.

-ot type: [v1.8+]
Select the data type for the output bands: Byte, Int16, UInt16, UInt32 Int32, Float32, Float64, CInt16, CInt32, CFloat32, CFloat64. Defaults to Float64.

-q: [v1.8+]
Suppress progress monitor and other non-error output.

src_datasource:
Any OGR supported readable datasource.[60]

[60] See Vector Data Formats chapter on page 337 for options.

dst_filename:
The GDAL supported output file. It must support update mode access. Before GDAL 1.8.0, gdal_rasterize could not create *new* output files and could only update existing ones.

Examples

Burn all polygons from (mask.shp) vector datasource into the RGB TIFF raster file (work.tif) with the color red (RGB = 255,0,0):

```
gdal_rasterize -b 1 -b 2 -b 3 -burn 255 -burn 0 -burn 0 \
                    -l mask mask.shp work.tif
```

Burn all features that have the attribute of class=A into the output elevation file, using the elevation from the ROOF_H attribute:

```
gdal_rasterize -a ROOF_H -where 'class="A"' \
                    -l footprints footprints.shp city_dem.tif
```

9

pct2rgb.py

> **Tips**
> - This is a Python script, and will only work if GDAL was built with Python support.
> - The new `-expand rgb|rgba` option of `gdal_translate` obsoletes this utility.

Syntax

```
pct2rgb.py [-of format] [-b band] [-rgba]
           source_file dest_file
```

Description

This utility will convert a pseudo-color band on the input file into an output RGB file of the desired format.

-of format:
:   Format to be generated (defaults to GeoTIFF).

-b band:
:   Band number to convert to RGB, defaults to 1.

-rgba:
Generate a RGBA file, with alpha band, instead of default RGB.

source_file:
The input GDAL supported raster file.

dest_file:
The output RGB raster file to be created.

10

rgb2pct.py

Tips
- This is a Python script, and will only work if GDAL was built with Python support.
- The new `-expand rgb|rgba` option of `gdal_translate` obsoletes this utility.

Syntax

```
rgb2pct.py [-n colors | -pct palette_file] [-of format]
           source_file dest_file
```

Description

This utility will compute an optimal pseudo-color table for a given RGB image using a median cut algorithm[61] on a downsampled RGB histogram. Then it converts the image into a pseudo-colored image using the color table.

This conversion utilizes Floyd-Steinberg dithering (error diffusion) to maximize output image visual quality.

[61] Median cut is an algorithm to sort data of an arbitrary number of dimensions into series of sets by cutting each set of data at the median point. Median cut is typically used for color quantization. For example, to reduce a 64k-colour image to 256 colours, median cut is used to find 256 colours that match the original data well. From http://wikipedia.org/wiki/Median_cut.

-n colors:
> Select the number of colors, between 2 and 256, to generate in the color table. Defaults to 256.

-pct palette_file:
> Extract the color table from *palette_file* instead of computing it. Can be used to have a consistent color table for multiple files.
>
> The *palette_file* must be a raster file in a GDAL supported format with a palette.

-of format:
> Format to generate (defaults to GeoTIFF). Same semantics as the -of flag for gdal_translate. Only output formats supporting pseudo-color tables should be used.

source_file:
> The input RGB GDAL raster file.

dest_file:
> The output pseudo-colored file that will be created.

Example

If it is desired to hand create the palette, likely the simplest text format is the GDAL VRT[62] format.

[62] VRT: http://loc8.cc/gdal_vrt

The following example VRT file, palette.vrt, was created in a text editor with a small 4 color palette with RGBA colors:

```
<VRTDataset rasterXSize="226" rasterYSize="271">
  <VRTRasterBand dataType="Byte" band="1">
    <ColorInterp>Palette</ColorInterp>
    <ColorTable>
      <Entry c1="238" c2="238" c3="238" c4="255"/>
      <Entry c1="237" c2="237" c3="237" c4="255"/>
      <Entry c1="236" c2="236" c3="236" c4="255"/>
      <Entry c1="229" c2="229" c3="229" c4="255"/>
    </ColorTable>
  </VRTRasterBand>
</VRTDataset>
```

EXAMPLE   153

Use the pseudo-color table from `palette.vrt`, to convert the input raster `rgb.tif` from RGB to PCT file `pseudo-colored.tif`:

```
rgb2pct.py -pct palette.vrt rgb.tif pseudo-colored.tif
```

11

gdaltransform

> **Tip**
> Input and output must always be in decimal form. There is
> currently no support for degree-minute-seconds (DMS) input
> or output.

Syntax

```
gdaltransform [--help-general] [-i]
              [-s_srs srs_def] [-t_srs srs_def]
              [-to "NAME=VALUE"]
              [-order n] [-tps] [-rpc] [-geoloc]
              [-gcp pixel line easting northing [elevation]]*
              [srcfile [dstfile]]
```

Description

The gdaltransform utility reprojects a list of coordinates into any
supported projection, including GCP-based transformations.

Coordinates are read as pairs (or triplets) of numbers per line from
standard input, transformed, and written out to standard output in

the same way. All transformations offered by gdalwarp are handled, including those based on GCPs.

Note that input and output must always be in decimal form. There is currently no support for DMS input or output.

If an input image file is provided, input is in pixel/line coordinates on that image. If an output file is provided, output is in pixel/line coordinates on that image.

Syntax

-s_srs *srs def:*
  Source spatial reference set. The coordinate systems that can be passed are anything supported by OGR which includes EPSG PCS and GCSes (i.e. EPSG:4296), PROJ.4 declarations, or the name of a .prj file containing well known text.

-t_srs *srs_def:*
  Target spatial reference set. The coordinate systems that can be passed are anything supported by OGR which includes EPSG PCS and GCSes (i.e. EPSG:4296), PROJ.4 declarations, or the name of a .prf file containing well known text.

-to *NAME=VALUE:*
  Set a transformer option suitable to pass to GDALCreateGenImg-ProjTransformer2().[63]

-order *n:*
  Order of polynomial used for warping (1 to 3). The default is to select a polynomial order based on the number of GCPs.

-tps:
  Force use of thin plate spline transformer based on available GCPs.

-rpc:
  Force use of RPCs.

-geoloc:
  Force use of Geolocation Arrays.

-i
  Inverse transformation: from destination to source.

[63] See http://loc8.cc/gdal_projtrans

-gcp pixel line easting northing [elevation]:
> Provide a GCP to be used for transformation (generally three or more are required).

srcfile:
> File with source projection definition or GCPs. If not given, source projection is read from the command-line `-s_srs` or `-gcp` parameters.

dstfile:
> File with destination projection definition.

Examples

Reprojection Example

Simple reprojection from one projected coordinate system to another:

```
gdaltransform -s_srs EPSG:28992 -t_srs EPSG:31370 \
              177502 311865
```

Produces the following output in meters in the "Belge 1972 / Belgian Lambert 72" projection:

```
244510.77404604 166154.532871342 -1046.79270555763
```

Image RPC Example

The following command requests an RPC-based transformation using the RPC model associated with the named file. Because the `-i` (inverse) flag is used, the transformation is from output georeferenced (WGS84) coordinates back to image coordinate:

```
gdaltransform -i -rpc 06OCT20025052_P001.TIF \
              125.67206 39.85307 50
```

Produces this output measured in pixels and lines on the image:

```
3499.49282422381 2910.83892848414 50
```

12

nearblack

Tips

- All processing is done in 8bit (Bytes)
- If the output file is omitted, results will be written back to the input file - which must support updates

Syntax

```
nearblack [-of format] [-white] [-near dist]
         [-nb non_black_pixels] [-setalpha]
         [-setmask] [-o outfile] [-q]
         [-co "NAME=VALUE"]* infile
```

Description

This utility will scan an image and try to set all pixels that are nearly black (or nearly white) around the collar to exactly black (or white). This is often used to "fix up" lossy compressed air photos so that color pixels can be treated as transparent when mosaicking.

-o outfile:
   The name of the output file to be created. Newly created files are created with the HFA driver by default (Erdas Imagine - .img)

-of format: [v1.8+]

Select the output GDAL format. Use the short format name (GTiff for GeoTIFF for example).[64]

-co "NAME=VALUE": [v1.8+]

Passes a creation option to the output format driver. Multiple -co options may be listed. See format-specific documentation for legal creation options for each format.

Only valid when creating a new file.

-white:

Search for nearly white (255) pixels instead of nearly black pixels.

-near dist:

Select threshold of how far from black (or white) the pixel values can be and still be considered near black (white). Defaults to 15.

-nb non_black_pixels:

Number of non-black pixels that can be encountered before giving up search inwards. Defaults to 2.

-setalpha: [v1.8+]

- Adds an alpha band if the output file is specified and the input file has 3 bands
- or sets the alpha band of the output file if it is specified and the input file has 4 bands
- or sets the alpha band of the input file if it has 4 bands and no output file is specified.

The alpha band is set to 0 in the image collar and to 255 elsewhere.

-setmask: [v1.8+]

Adds a mask band to the output file, or adds a mask band to the input file if it does not already have one and no output file is specified. The mask band is set to 0 in the image collar and to 255 elsewhere.

-q: [v1.8+]

Suppress progress monitor and other non-error output.

infile:

The input file. Any GDAL supported format, any number of

bands, normally 8bit Byte bands.

The algorithm processes the image one scanline at a time. A scan "in" is done from either end setting pixels to black until at least *non_black_pixels* (-nb) pixels that are more than *dist* gray levels (-near) away from black have been encountered at which point the scan stops. The nearly black pixels are set to black. The algorithm also scans from top to bottom and from bottom to top to identify indentations in the top or bottom.

13

gdal_merge

> **Tip**
>
> This is a Python script, and will only work if GDAL was built with Python support.

Syntax

```
gdal_merge.py [-o out_filename] [-of out_format]
              [-co NAME=VALUE]* [-ps pixelsize_x pixelsize_y]
              [-tap] [-separate] [-v] [-pct]
              [-ul_lr ulx uly lrx lry] [-n nodata_value]
              [-init "value [value...]"] [-ot datatype]
              [-createonly] input_files
```

Description

This utility will automatically mosaic a set of images. All the images must be in the same coordinate system and have a matching number of bands, but they may be overlapping and at different resolutions. In areas of overlap, the last image will be copied over earlier ones.

-o out_filename:
   The name of the output file, which will be created if it does not

already exist. Defaults to out.tif.

-of *format:*

Output format, defaults to GeoTIFF (GTiff).

-co *NAME=VALUE:*

Creation option for output file. Multiple options can be specified.

-ot *datatype:*

Force the output image bands to have a specific type. Use type names (i.e. Byte, Int16,...).

-ps *pixelsize_x pixelsize_y:*

Pixel size to be used for the output file. If not specified the resolution of the first input file will be used.

-tap: *[v1.8+]*

Target Aligned Pixels - align the coordinates of the extent of the output file to the values of the -tr, such that the aligned extent includes the minimum extent.

-ul_lr *ulx uly lrx lry:*

The extents of the output file. If not specified the aggregate extents of all input files will be used.

-v:

Generate verbose output of mosaicking operations as they are done.

-separate:

Place each input file into a separate *stacked* band.

-pct:

Grab a pseudo-color table from the first input image, and use it for the output. Merging pseudo-colored images this way assumes that all input files use the same color table.

-n *nodata_value:*

Ignore pixels from files being merged in with this pixel value.

-init *"value(s)":*

Pre-initialize the output image bands with these values. However, it is not marked as the nodata value in the output file. If only one value is given, the same value is used in all the bands.

EXAMPLE 165

-createonly:
> The output file is created (and potentially pre-initialized) but no input image data is copied into it.

Example

Create an image with the pixels in all bands initialized to 255 and specifying two input TIFF files:

```
gdal_merge.py -init 255 -o out.tif in1.tif in2.tif
```

Create an RGB image that shows blue in pixels with no data. The first two bands will be initialized to 0 and the third band will be initialized to 255:

```
gdal_merge.py -init "0 0 255" -o out.tif in1.tif in2.tif
```

14

gdal2tiles

> **Tip**
>
> This is a Python script that needs to be run against "new generation" Python GDAL bindings [v1.7+]

Syntax

```
gdal2tiles.py [-p profile] [-r resampling]
              [-s srs] [-z zoom] [-e]
              [-a nodata] [-v] [-h] [-k] [-n] [-u url]
              [-w webviewer] [-t title] [-c copyright]
              [-g googlekey] [-b bingkey]
              input_file [output_dir]
```

Description

This utility takes an input GDAL raster file and generates a directory with small tiles and metadata, following the OSGeo[65] Tile Map Service (TMS) specification.[66]

Simple web pages with viewers based on Google Maps and Open-Layers are generated as well—so anybody can comfortably explore

---

[65] OSGeo: http://loc8.cc/osgeo

[66] TMS: http://loc8.cc/tms

your maps on-line and you do not need to install or configure any special software (like MapServer[67]) and the map displays very fast in the web browser. You only need to upload the generated directory to a web server.

gdal2tiles also creates the necessary metadata for Google Earth (KML SuperOverlay), but only if the supplied map uses EPSG:4326 projection.

World files and embedded georeferencing is used during tile generation, but you can publish a picture without proper georeferencing too.

-p *PROFILE, –profile=PROFILE:*
Tile cutting profile (mercator,geodetic,raster) - default 'mercator' (Google Maps compatible). Use raster for non-georeferenced source images.

-r *RESAMPLING, –resampling=RESAMPLING:*
Resampling method (average,near,bilinear,cubic,cubicspline,lanczos,antialias - default 'average'.

-s *SRS, --s_srs=SRS:*
The spatial reference system used for the source input data.

-z *ZOOM, --zoom=ZOOM:*
Zoom levels to render (format:'2-5' or '10').

-e, *--resume:*
Resume mode. Generate only missing files.

-a *NODATA, --srcnodata=NODATA:*
NODATA transparency value to assign to the input data.

-v, *--verbose:*
Generate verbose output of tile generation.

-h, *--help:*
Show help message and exit.

--version:
Show program's version number and exit.

input_file:

> Input GDAL supported file as source of output tiles.

output_dir:

> Output directory for storing the tiles produced.

KML (Google Earth) options

Options for generated Google Earth SuperOverlay metadata:

-k, --force-kml:

> Generate KML for Google Earth - default for 'geodetic' profile and 'raster' in EPSG:4326. For a dataset with different projection use with caution!

-n, --no-kml:

> Avoid automatic generation of KML files for EPSG:4326.

-u URL, --url=URL:

> URL address where the generated tiles are going to be published.

Web viewer options

Options for generated HTML viewers a la Google Maps

-w WEBVIEWER, --webviewer=WEBVIEWER:

> Web viewer to generate (all,google,openlayers,none) - default 'all'.

-t TITLE, --title=TITLE:

> Title used for generated metadata, web viewers and KML files.

-c COPYRIGHT, --copyright=COPYRIGHT:

> Copyright for the map.

-g GOOGLEKEY, --googlekey=GOOGLEKEY:

> Google Maps API key from http://code.google.com/apis/maps/ signup.html.

-b BINGKEY, --bingkey=BINGKEY:

> Bing Maps API key from https://www.bingmapsportal.com/

input_file:

> Input GDAL supported file as source of output tiles.

output_dir:

> Output directory for storing the tiles produced.

Reference

- Developers at Klokan:
  `http://www.klokan.cz/projects/gdal2tiles/`
- KML and gdal2tiles tutorial:
  `https://developers.google.com/kml/articles/raster`

15

gdal-config

REPORTS GDAL INSTALLATION INFORMATION

> **Tip**
>
> Available on Unix-based systems

Syntax

```
gdal-config [--prefix[=DIR]]
            [--libs]
            [--cflags]
            [--version]
            [--ogr-enabled]
            [--formats]
```

Description

This utility script (available on Unix systems) can be used to determine various information about a GDAL installation. It is normally used by configuration scripts for applications using GDAL, but can also be queried by an end user.

> *--prefix*:
> The top level directory for the GDAL installation.

--libs:

The libraries and link directives required to use GDAL.

--cflags:

The include and macro definition required to compiled modules using GDAL.

--version:

Reports the GDAL version.

--ogr-enabled:

Reports (yes/no) whether OGR is built into GDAL.

--formats:

Reports which raster formats are configured into GDAL.

16

gdal_retile.py

RETILE A SET OF TILES AND/OR BUILD TILED PYRAMID LEVELS

Tips

- This is a Python script, and will only work if GDAL was built with Python support.
- If your number of input tiles exhausts the command line buffer, use the general --optfile option.

Syntax

```
gdal_retile.py [-v] [-co NAME=VALUE] [-of out_format]
           [-ps pixelWidth pixelHeight] [-ot  type]
           [ -tileIndex idxName [-tileIndexField fldName]]
           [ -csv fileName [-csvDelim delimiter]]
           [-s_srs srs_def]  [-pyramidOnly]
           [-r {near/bilinear/cubic/cubicspline/lanczos}]
           -levels numberoflevels
           [-useDirForEachRow]
           -targetDir TileDirectory
           input_files
```

Description

This utility will retile a set of input tile(s). All the input tile(s) must be georeferenced in the same coordinate system and have a matching number of bands. Pyramid levels must also be generated. It is possible to generate shapefile(s) for the tiled output.

-of *format:*
: Output format, defaults to GeoTIFF (GTiff).

-co *NAME=VALUE:*
: Creation option for output file. Multiple options may be specified.

-ot *type:*
: Select the data type for the output bands: Byte, Int16, UInt16, UInt32 Int32, Float32, Float64, CInt16, CInt32, CFloat32, CFloat64.

-ps *pixelsize_x pixelsize_y:*
: Pixel size to be used for the output file. Default is 256 x 256.

-levels numberOfLevels:
: Number of pyramid levels to build.

-v:
: Generate verbose output of tile operations as they are done.

-pyramidOnly:
: No retiling, build only the pyramids.

-r *algorithm:*
: Resampling algorithm, options are: near, bilinear, cubic, cubic-spline, lanczos. Default is near.

-s_srs *srs_def:*
: Source spatial reference to use. The coordinate systems that can be passed are anything supported by OGR which includes EPSG PCS and GCSes (i.e.EPSG:4296), PROJ.4 declarations (as above), or the name of a .prf file containing well known text.

: If no *srs_def* is given, the *srs_def* of the source tiles is used (if there is any). The *srs_def* will be propagated to created tiles (if possible) and to the optional shapefile(s).

-tileIndex *idxName:*
: The name of the shapefile to create for each tile index.

-tileIndexField fldName:
> The name of the attribute containing the tile name.

-csv csvFileName:
> The name of the CSV file containing the tile georeferencing infor-
> mation. The file contains 5 columns:
>
>  ```
>  tilename,minx,maxx,miny,maxy
>  ```

-csvDelim column delimiter:
> The column delimiter used in the CSV file. Default is semicolon
> (;).

-useDirForEachRow:
> Normally the tiles of the base image are stored as described in
> `-targetDir`. For large images, some file systems have performance
> problems if the number of files in a directory is too big, causing
> `gdal_retile.py` not to finish in reasonable time. Using this pa-
> rameter creates a different output structure.
>
> The tiles of the base image are stored in a subdirectory called `0`, the
> pyramids in subdirectories are numbered `1,2,....` Within each of
> these directories another level of subdirectories is created, num-
> bered `0...n`, depending of how many tile rows are needed for
> each level. Finally, a directory contains only the tiles for one row
> for a specific level.
>
> For large images a performance improvement of a factor N could
> be achieved.

-targetDir directory:
> The directory where the tile result is created. Pyramids are stored
> in subdirectories numbered from `1`. Created tile names have a
> numbering schema and contain the name of the source tiles.

input_files:
> Input filenames, must be supported GDAL format files. If your
> number of input tiles exhausts the command line buffer, use the
> general `--optfile` option.

Examples

Basic default behaviour produces a folder of multiple tiled pieces
of the source raster. In this case, take a global image and produces

tiles in an existing folder:

```
gdal_retile.py -targetDir output_dir NE1_50M_SR_W/NE1_50M_SR_W.tif
```

This produces 946 files in the output_dir folder. The source image was chopped into 22 rows and 43 columns. Figure 16.1 shows a preview of some of these files in the OS X Finder.

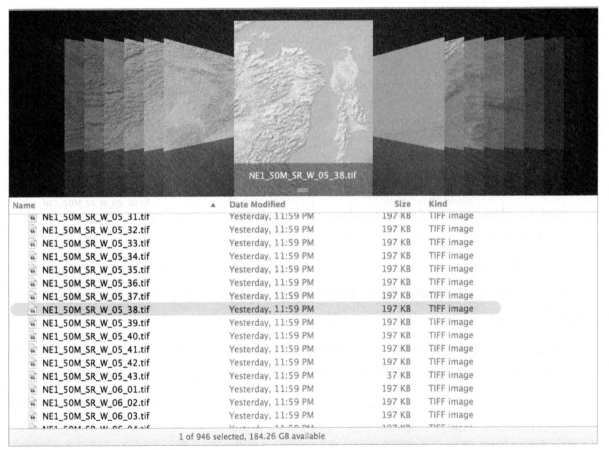

Figure 16.1: gdal_retile default output tile examples

Looking at the default results shows that the original coordinate system data is retained and that the default tile size was 256x256:

```
gdalinfo output_dir/NE1_50M_SR_W_01_01.tif
```

```
Driver: GTiff/GeoTIFF
Files: output_dir/NE1_50M_SR_W_01_01.tif
Size is 256, 256
...
```

That target output tile size can be modified using the -ps option, for example, changing the output size to 128x128 pixels for each tile:

```
gdal_retile.py -ps 128 128 -targetDir output_dir \
               NE1_50M_SR_W/NE1_50M_SR_W.tif
```

Generating pyramids from multiple tiles is also possible. In this case, you specify the source files, using wildcards, from the previous step and select the -pyramidOnly option:

```
gdal_retile.py -pyramidOnly -levels 4 -ps 1024 1024 -targetDir output_pyr \
               output_dir/*.tif
```

This produces 4 new output subfolders, with varying levels of pyramid tiles in each. Level 1 folder is the largest scale, level 4 is smallest, but shows the entire source image. In all cases, the max tile size was 1024 wide/high:

```
$ ls output_pyr
1    2       3       4

$ ls output_pyr/1
NE1_50M_SR_W_01_01_1_1.tif  NE1_50M_SR_W_01_01_1_5.tif
NE1_50M_SR_W_01_01_1_2.tif  NE1_50M_SR_W_01_01_1_6.tif
NE1_50M_SR_W_01_01_1_3.tif  NE1_50M_SR_W_01_01_2_1.tif
NE1_50M_SR_W_01_01_1_4.tif  NE1_50M_SR_W_01_01_2_2.tif
...

$ ls output_pyr/4
NE1_50M_SR_W_01_01_1_1.tif
```

Figure 16.2, on the next page shows a preview of a level 1 and level 4 tile.

Figure 16.2: Files created by pyramid option
from source tiles

17

gdal_grid

Syntax

```
gdal_grid [-ot type] [-of format] [-co "NAME=VALUE"]
        [-zfield field_name] [-a_srs srs_def]
        [-spat xmin ymin xmax ymax]
        [-clipsrc <xmin ymin xmax ymax>|WKT|datasource|spat_extent]
        [-clipsrcsql sql_statement]  [-clipsrclayer layer]
        [-clipsrcwhere expression]
        [-l layername]*
        [-where expression] [-sql select_statement]
        [-txe xmin xmax] [-tye ymin ymax]
        [-outsize xsize ysize]
        [-a algorithm[:parameter1=value1]*] [-q]
        src_datasource dst_filename
```

Description

This program creates a regular raster grid from scattered/irregular data read from an OGR datasource. Input data will be interpolated[68] to fill grid cells with values and you can choose from various interpolation methods (see Interpolation Algorithms below).

---

[68] For more on interpolation concepts see Wikipedia: http://loc8.cc/gpt/interpolate

Default Algorithms and Metric Settings

Default values for the available algorithms are as follows—also see the Interpolation Algorithms and Data Metrics sections below for more details:

Inverse Distance to a Power (default algorithm):

```
invdist:power=2.0:smoothing=0.0:radius1=0.0: \
         radius2=0.0:angle=0.0:max_points=0: \
         min_points=0:nodata=0.0
```

Moving Average:

```
average:radius1=0.0:radius2=0.0:angle=0.0: \
         min_points=0:nodata=0.0
```

Nearest Neighbor:

```
nearest:radius1=0.0:radius2=0.0:angle=0.0:nodata=0.0
```

Data Metrics:

```
<metric name>:radius1=0.0:radius2=0.0:angle=0.0: \
                min_points=0:nodata=0.0
```

-ot *type:*
Select the data type for the output bands: Byte, Int16, UInt16, UInt32 Int32, Float32, Float64, CInt16, CInt32, CFloat32, CFloat64.

-of *format:*
Select the output format. The default is GeoTIFF (GTiff). Use the short format name.

-txe *xmin xmax:*
Set georeferenced X extents of output file to be created.

-tye *ymin ymax:*
Set georeferenced Y extents of output file to be created.

-outsize *xsize ysize:*
Set the size of the output file in pixels and lines.

-a_srs *srs_def:*
Override the projection for the output file. The *srs_def* may be any of the usual GDAL/OGR forms, complete WKT, PROJ.4, EPSG:n or a file containing the WKT.

-zfield *field_name:*
Identifies an attribute field on the features to be used to get a Z value from. This value overrides Z value read from feature geometry record (naturally, if you have a Z value in geometry, otherwise you have no choice and should specify a field name containing Z value).

-a *[algorithm[:parameter1=value1][:parameter2=value2]...]:*
Set the interpolation algorithm or data metric name and (optionally) its parameters. See Interpolation Algorithms and Data Metrics sections below for further discussion of available options.

-spat *xmin ymin xmax ymax:*
Adds a spatial filter to select only features contained within the bounding box described by *(xmin, ymin) - (xmax, ymax)*.

-clipsrc *[xmin ymin xmax ymax] | WKT | datasource | spat_extent:*
Adds a spatial filter to select only features contained within the specified bounding box (expressed in source SRS), WKT geometry (POLYGON or MULTIPOLYGON), from a datasource or to the spatial extent of the -spat option if you use the *spat_extent* keyword.

When specifying a datasource, you will generally want to use it in combination with the -clipsrclayer, -clipsrcwhere or -clipsrcsql options.

-clipsrcsql *sql_statement:*
Select desired geometries using an SQL query instead.

-clipsrclayer *layername:*
Select the named layer from the source clip datasource.

-clipsrcwhere *expression:*
Restrict desired geometries based on attribute query.

-l *layername:*
Indicates the layer(s) from the datasource that will be used for input features. May be specified multiple times, but at least one layer name or a -sql option must be specified.

-where *expression:*
An optional SQL WHERE-style query expression to be applied to select features to process from the input layer(s).

-sql select_statement:
    An SQL statement to be evaluated against the datasource to pro-
    duce a virtual layer of features to be processed.

-co "NAME=VALUE":
    Passes a creation option to the output format driver. Multiple -co
    options may be listed. See format specific documentation for legal
    creation options for each format.

-q:
    Suppress progress monitor and other non-error output.

src_datasource:
    Any OGR supported readable datasource.

dst_filename:
    The GDAL supported output file.

Interpolation Algorithms

There are a number of interpolation algorithms to choose from: in-
vdist, average, nearest.

invdist

Inverse distance to a power. This is the default algorithm. It has the
following parameters:

power:
    Weighting power. Default is 2.0.

smoothing:
    Smoothing parameter. Default is 0.0.

radius1:
    The first radius (X axis if rotation angle is 0) of search ellipse. Set
    this parameter to zero to use the whole point array. Default is 0.0.

radius2:
    The second radius (Y axis if rotation angle is 0) of search ellipse.
    Set this parameter to zero to use the whole point array. Default is
    0.0.

angle:

Angle of search ellipse rotation, measured counter-clockwise, in degrees. Default is 0.0.

max_points:

Maximum number of data points to use. Do not search for more points than this number. This is only used if search ellipse is set (both radiuses are non-zero). Zero means that all found points should be used. Default is 0.

min_points:

Minimum number of data points to use. If less amount of points found the grid node is considered empty and will be filled with NODATA markers. This is only used if search ellipse is set (both radiuses are non-zero). Default is 0.

nodata:

NODATA marker to fill empty points. Default is 0.0.

average

Moving average algorithm. It has the following parameters:

radius1:

The first radius (X axis if rotation angle is 0) of search ellipse. Set this parameter to zero to use the whole point array. Default is 0.0.

radius2:

The second radius (Y axis if rotation angle is 0) of search ellipse. Set this parameter to zero to use the whole point array. Default is 0.0.

angle:

Angle of search ellipse rotation, measured counter-clockwise, in degrees. Default is 0.0.

min_points:

Minimum number of data points to use. If fewer points are found the grid node is considered empty and will be filled with NO-DATA marker. Default is 0.

nodata:

NODATA marker to fill empty points. Default is 0.0.

Note, that it is essential to set search ellipse when using the moving average method. It is a window that will be averaged when computing grid node values.

nearest

Nearest neighbour algorithm. It has the following parameters:

radius1:
The first radius (X axis if rotation angle is 0) of search ellipse. Set this parameter to zero to use the whole point array. Default is 0.0.

radius2:
The second radius (Y axis if rotation angle is 0) of search ellipse. Set this parameter to zero to use the whole point array. Default is 0.0.

angle:
Angle of search ellipse rotation, measured counter-clockwise, in degrees. Default is 0.0.

nodata:
NODATA marker to fill empty points. Default is 0.0.

Data Metrics

Besides the interpolation functionality, gdal_grid can be used to compute some data metrics using the specified window and output grid geometry. These metrics are:

minimum:
Minimum value found in grid node search ellipse.

maximum:
Maximum value found in grid node search ellipse.

range:
A difference between the minimum and maximum values found in grid node search ellipse.

count:
A number of data points found in grid node search ellipse.

average_distance:
> An average distance between the grid node (center of the search ellipse) and all of the data points found in grid node search ellipse.

average_distance_pts:
> An average distance between the data points found in grid node search ellipse. The distance between each pair of points within ellipse is calculated and average of all distances is set as a grid node value.

Data Metric Options

All the metrics have the same set of options:

radius1:
> The first radius (X axis if rotation angle is 0) of search ellipse. Set this parameter to zero to use the whole point array. Default is 0.0.

radius2:
> The second radius (Y axis if rotation angle is 0) of search ellipse. Set this parameter to zero to use the whole point array. Default is 0.0.

angle:
> Angle of search ellipse rotation, measured counter-clockwise, in degrees. Default is 0.0.

min_points:
> Minimum number of data points to use. If fewer points are found the grid node is considered empty and will be filled with NO-DATA marker. This is only used if search ellipse is set (both radiuses are non-zero). Default is 0.

nodata:
> NODATA marker to fill empty points. Default is 0.0.

Reading Comma Separated Values

Often you have a text file with a list of comma separated XYZ values to work with (known as a CSV file). You can easily use that kind of data source in gdal_grid. All you need to do is create a virtual dataset header (VRT) for your CSV file and use it as the input datasource for `gdal_grid`. You can find more details on the VRT format online.[69]

Here is a small example, a CSV file named `dem.csv`:

```
Easting,Northing,Elevation
86943.4,891957,139.13
87124.3,892075,135.01
86962.4,892321,182.04
87077.6,891995,135.01
...
```

Create a `dem.vrt` virtual layer file, pointing to the above `dem.csv` CSV file:

```
<OGRVRTDataSource>
  <OGRVRTLayer name="dem">
    <SrcDataSource>dem.csv</SrcDataSource>
    <GeometryType>wkbPoint</GeometryType>
    <GeometryField encoding="PointFromColumns"
              x="Easting" y="Northing" z="Elevation"/>
  </OGRVRTLayer>
</OGRVRTDataSource>
```

This description specifies what is known as a 2.5D geometry with three coordinates X, Y and Z. The Z value will be used for interpolation. Your `dem.vrt` can now be used with all OGR programs (start with `ogrinfo` to test that everything works fine).

The datasource will contain a single layer called `dem` filled with point features constructed from values in the CSV file. Using this technique you can handle CSV files with more than three columns, switch columns, etc.

If your CSV file does not contain column headers then it can be handled in the following way:

```
<GeometryField encoding="PointFromColumns"
          x="field_1" y="field_2" z="field_3"/>
```

The Comma Separated Value description page[70] contains details on the CSV format supported by GDAL/OGR.

[70] http://loc8.cc/ogr_csv

Examples

Create a raster TIFF file from the VRT datasource, described above, using the inverse distance to a power method. Values to interpolate will be read from the Z value of the geometry record:

```
gdal_grid -a invdist:power=2.0:smoothing=1.0
          -txe 85000 89000
          -tye 894000 890000 -outsize 400 400 -of GTiff
          -ot Float64 -l dem
          dem.vrt dem.tiff
```

This next example is similar, but reads values to interpolate from the attribute field specified with the -zfield option instead of the geometry record. In this case X and Y coordinates are being taken from geometry and Z is being taken from the Elevation field:

```
gdal_grid -zfield "Elevation"
          -a invdist:power=2.0:smoothing=1.0 -txe 85000 89000
          -tye 894000 890000 -outsize 400 400 -of GTiff
          -ot Float64 -l dem
          dem.vrt dem.tiff
```

18

gdaldem

ANALYZE AND VISUALIZE DIGITAL ELEVATION MODELS (DEM)

Contents

Syntax

```
gdaldem mode input_dem output_xxx_map
        [-of format]
        [-compute_edges]
        [-alg ZevenbergenThorne]
        [-b band]
        [-co "NAME=VALUE"]
        [-q]
        [mode-specific options]
```

Description

The gdaldem command was first introduced in GDAL 1.7.

The following general options are available :

mode:
> Select the output map algorithm mode to be used. Options include: `hillshade`, `slope`, `aspect`, `color-relief`, `TRI`, `TPI`, `roughness`. See Mode Details section below for more details on each mode and their options.

input_dem:
> The input DEM raster file to be processed.

output_xxx_map:
> The output raster file to be produced.

-of format:
> Select the output raster file format. The default is GeoTIFF (GTiff). Use the short format name.[71]

-compute_edges: [v1.8+]
> Do the computation at raster edges and near nodata values.

-alg ZevenbergenThorne: [v1.8+]
> Use Zevenbergen & Thorne formula, instead of Horn's formula, to compute slope & aspect. The literature suggests Zevenbergen & Thorne to be more suited to smooth landscapes, whereas Horn's formula to perform better on rougher terrain.

-b band:
> Select an input *band* number to be processed. Bands are numbered starting from 1.

-co "NAME=VALUE":
> Passes a creation option to the output format driver. Multiple `-co` options may be listed. See format specific documentation for legal creation options for each format.

-q:
> Suppress progress monitor and other non-error output.

For all algorithms, except color-relief, a nodata value in the target dataset will be emitted if at least one pixel set to the nodata value is found in the 3x3 window centered around each source pixel. The

[71] See the Raster Data Formats section on page 331 for list of formats.

consequence is that there will be a 1-pixel border around each image set with nodata value.

From GDAL 1.8.0, if -compute_edges is specified, gdaldem will compute values at image edges or if a nodata value is found in the 3x3 window, by interpolating missing values.

Mode Details

Summary of syntax for each mode is provided, followed by detailed syntax of each mode and its options.

All modes can generate output from any GDAL-supported elevation raster.

Hillshade - Shaded Relief

To generate a shaded relief map:

```
gdaldem hillshade input_dem output_hillshade
        [-z ZFactor (default=1)] [-s scale (default=1)]
        [-az Azimuth (default=315)]
        [-alt Altitude (default=45)]
        [-alg ZevenbergenThorne]
        [-compute_edges] [-b Band (default=1)]
        [-of format] [-co "NAME=VALUE"]* [-q]
```

This command outputs an 8-bit raster with a nice shaded relief effect. It's very useful for visualizing the terrain. You can optionally specify the azimuth and altitude of the light source, a vertical exaggeration factor and a scaling factor to account for differences between vertical and horizontal units.

The value 0 is used as the output nodata value.

The following specific options are available :

-z zFactor:
  Vertical exaggeration used to pre-multiply the elevations. Default is 1.

-s scale:

Ratio of vertical units to horizontal. If the horizontal unit of the source DEM is degrees (e.g Lat/Long WGS84 projection), you can use the scale setting of -s 111120 if the vertical units are meters (or 370400 if they are in feet). Default is 1.

-az azimuth:

Azimuth/bearing of the light, in degrees; 0 if it comes from the top/north of the raster, 90 from the east, etc. The default value, 315, should rarely be changed as it is the value generally used to generate shaded maps.

-alt altitude:

Altitude of the light, in degrees, where 90 sets the light to come from directly above the DEM, 0 for light coming from the level of the horizon. Default is 45 degrees.

Slope

To generate a slope map:

```
gdaldem slope input_dem output_slope_map
        [-p use percent slope (default=degrees)]
        [-s scale* (default=1)]
        [-alg ZevenbergenThorne]
        [-compute_edges] [-b Band (default=1)]
        [-of format] [-co "NAME=VALUE"]* [-q]
```

This command will take a DEM raster and output a 32-bit float raster with slope values. You have the option of specifying the type of slope value you want: degrees or percent slope. In cases where the horizontal units differ from the vertical units, you can also supply a scaling factor.

The value -9999 is used as the output nodata value.

The following specific options are available :

-p:

If specified, the slope will be expressed as percent slope. Otherwise, it is expressed as degrees by default. Slope is defined as the ratio between rise/run or height/length.

-s scale:
> Ratio of vertical units to horizontal. If the horizontal unit of the source DEM is degrees (e.g Lat/Long WGS84 projection), you can use the scale setting of `-s 111120` if the vertical units are meters (or `370400` if they are in feet). Default is 1.

Aspect

Generate an aspect map. Outputs a 32-bit float raster with pixel values from 0-360 indicating azimuth:

```
gdaldem aspect input_dem output_aspect_map
        [-trigonometric] [-zero_for_flat]
        [-alg ZevenbergenThorne]
        [-compute_edges] [-b Band (default=1)]
        [-of format] [-co "NAME=VALUE"]* [-q]
```

This command outputs a 32-bit float raster with values between 0 and 360 degrees, representing the azimuth/bearing that slopes are facing. The definition of the azimuth is such that: 0 means that the slope is facing the North, 90 is East, 180 is South and 270 is West (provided that the top of your input raster is north oriented).

The aspect value `-9999` is used as the nodata value to indicate undefined aspect in flat areas where slope is `0`.

The following specific options are available :

-trigonometric:
> Return trigonometric angle instead of azimuth. Thus 0 means East, 90 North, 180 West, 270 South.

-zero_for_flat:
> Return 0 for flat areas where slope is 0, instead of the `-9999` default.

Color Relief

Generate a color-relief map:

```
gdaldem color-relief input_dem
        color_text_file output_color_relief_map
```

```
[-alpha] [-exact_color_entry | -nearest_color_entry]
[-b Band (default=1)]
[-of format] [-co "NAME=VALUE"]* [-q]
```

This command outputs a 3-band (RGB) or 4-band (RGBA) raster with values computed from the elevation and a text-based color configuration file, containing the association between elevation values and the desired color.

By default, the colors between the given elevation values are blended smoothly and the result is a nice colorized DEM. To avoid linear interpolation for values that don't match an index of the color configuration file use either the -exact_color_entry or -nearest_color_entry option.

The following specific options are available:

color_text_file:
Specify the text-based color configuration file, contains lines of the format:

```
elevation_value red green blue
```

-alpha:
Add an alpha channel to the output raster.

-exact_color_entry:
Use strict matching when searching in the color configuration file. If no matching color entry is found, the 0,0,0,0 RGBA quadruplet will be used.

-nearest_color_entry:
Use the RGBA quadruplet corresponding to the closest entry in the color configuration file.

The color-relief mode is the only mode that supports VRT[72] as an output format. In that case, it will translate the color configuration file into appropriate <LUT> elements in the resulting VRT/XML. The VRT will also point to the source DEM file, without having to actually convert any physical file.

Note that elevations specified as percentage will be translated as absolute values, which must be taken into account when the statistics of the source raster differ from the one that was used when building the VRT.

This mode acts in a similar manner to the GRASS GIS r.shaded.relief functionality.[73]

[73] GRASS GIS Shaded Relief documentation: http://loc8.cc/grass_r_relief

The text-based color configuration file generally contains 4 columns per line: the elevation value and the corresponding Red, Green, Blue components (between 0 and 255).

The elevation value can be any floating point value, or the nv keyword for the nodata value. The elevation can also be expressed as a percentage: 0 being the minimum value found in the raster, 100 the maximum value.

An extra column can be optionally added for the alpha component. If it is not specified, full opacity (255) is assumed.

Various field separators are accepted: comma, tab, spaces, colon (:).

Common colors used by GRASS GIS can also be specified by using their name, instead of the RGB triplet. The supported list is: white, black, red, green, blue, yellow, magenta, cyan, aqua, grey/gray, orange, brown, purple/violet and indigo.

GMT .cpt palette files are also supported (COLOR_MODEL = RGB only). [v1.8+]

Note: the syntax of the color configuration file is derived from the one supported by the GRASS GIS r.colors utility.[74]

[74] GRASS GIS color name documentation: http://loc8.cc/grass_r_colors

ESRI HDR color table files (.clr) also match that syntax. The alpha component and the support of tab and comma as separators are GDAL-specific extensions.

Palette File Example:

```
3500    white
```

```
2500    235:220:175
50%     190 185 135
700     240 250 150
0        50 180  50
nv        0   0   0   0
```

Terrain Ruggedness Index (TRI)

Generate a Terrain Ruggedness Index (TRI) map from any GDAL-supported elevation raster:

```
gdaldem TRI input_dem output_TRI_map
        [-compute_edges] [-b Band (default=1)]
        [-of format] [-q]
```

This command outputs a single-band raster with values computed from the elevation. TRI stands for Terrain Ruggedness Index, which is defined as the mean difference between a central pixel and its surrounding cells (see Wilson et al 2007, Marine Geodesy 30:3-35).

The value -9999 is used as the output nodata value.

Topographic Position Index (TPI)

Generate a Topographic Position Index (TPI) map from any GDAL-supported elevation raster:

```
gdaldem TPI input_dem output_TPI_map
        [-compute_edges] [-b Band (default=1)]
        [-of format] [-q]
```

This command outputs a single-band raster with values computed from the elevation. TPI stands for Topographic Position Index, which is defined as the difference between a central pixel and the mean of its surrounding cells (see Wilson et al 2007, Marine Geodesy 30:3-35).

The value -9999 is used as the output nodata value.

Roughness

Generate a roughness map from any GDAL-supported elevation raster:

```
gdaldem roughness input_dem output_roughness_map
        [-compute_edges] [-b Band (default=1)]
        [-of format] [-q]
```

This command outputs a single-band raster with values computed from the elevation. Roughness is the largest inter-cell difference of a central pixel and its surrounding cells, as defined in Wilson et al (2007, Marine Geodesy 30:3-35).

The value -9999 is used as the output nodata value.

Authors

The gdaldem code and documentation were contributed by: Matthew Perry, Even Rouault, Howard Butler, Chris Yesson

Derived from code by:

Michael Shapiro, Olga Waupotitsch, Marjorie Larson, Jim Westervelt

In U.S. Army CERL, 1993. GRASS 4.1 Reference Manual. U.S. Army Corps of Engineers, Construction Engineering Research Laboratories, Champaign, Illinois, 1-425.

19

gdal_sieve.py

REMOVES SMALL RASTER POLYGONS

Syntax

```
gdal_sieve.py [-q] [-st threshold] [-4] [-8]
                [-o name=value]
                srcfile
                [-nomask] [-mask filename]
                [-of format] [dstfile]
```

Description

The gdal_sieve.py script removes raster polygons/slivers smaller than a provided threshold size (in pixels) and replaces them with the pixel value of the largest neighbour polygon. The result can be written back to the existing raster band, or copied into a new file.

Additional details on the algorithm are available in the GDALSieveFilter() API docs.[75]

[75] http://loc8.cc/gdal_sieve

-*q:*
   Run the script in quiet mode. The progress monitor is suppressed and routine messages are not displayed.

-st threshold:
Set the size threshold in pixels. Only raster polygons smaller than this size will be removed.

-o name=value:
Specify a special argument to the algorithm. Currently none are supported.

-4:
Four connectedness should be used when determining polygons. That is, diagonal pixels are not considered directly connected. This is the default.

-8:
Eight connectedness should be used when determining polygons. That is, diagonal pixels are considered directly connected.

srcfile
The source raster file used to identify target pixels. Only the first band is used.

-nomask:
Do not use the default validity mask for the input band (such as nodata, or alpha masks).

-mask filename:
Use the first band of the specified file as a validity mask (zero is invalid, non-zero is valid).

dstfile
The new file to create with the filtered result. If not provided, the source band is updated in place.

-of format:
Select the output format. The default is GeoTIFF (GTiff). Use the short format name.

20

gdallocationinfo

Syntax

```
gdallocationinfo [--help-general] [-xml] [-lifonly]
                 [-valonly] [-b band]*
                 [-l_srs srs_def] [-geoloc] [-wgs84]
                 srcfile [x y]
```

Description

The gdallocationinfo utility provides a mechanism to query information about a pixel at a given location in one of a variety of coordinate systems. Several reporting options are provided.

-*xml:*
> The output report will be XML formatted for convenient post-processing.

-*lifonly:*
> Only output filenames that include values returned from the LocationInfo request against the database (i.e. for identifying impacted file from VRT).

-*valonly:*
> Only output the pixel values of the selected pixel on each of the

selected bands.

-b band:
Selects a band to query. Multiple bands can be listed. By default all bands are queried.

-l_srs srs def:
The coordinate system of the input location.

-geoloc:
Indicates that input points are in the georeferencing system of the image.

-wgs84:
Indicates that input points are WGS84 (lat/long).

srcfile:
The source GDAL raster file name.

x:
X location of target pixel. By default the coordinate system is pixel/line unless -l_srs, -wgs84 or -geoloc are supplied.

y:
Y location of target pixel. By default the coordinate system is pixel/line unless -l_srs, -wgs84 or -geoloc are supplied.

This utility is intended to provide a variety of information about a pixel. Currently it reports:

- The location of the pixel in pixel/line space
- The result of a LocationInfo metadata query against the datasource - currently this is only implemented for VRT files which will report the file(s) used to satisfy requests for that pixel
- The raster pixel value of that pixel for all, or a subset of, the bands
- The unscaled pixel value if a Scale and/or Offset apply to the band

The pixel selected is requested by x/y coordinate on the command line, or read from stdin. More than one coordinate pair can be supplied when reading coordinates from stdin.

By default pixel/line coordinates are expected. However, with use of the -geoloc, -wgs84, or -l_srs switches it is possible to specify the location in other coordinate systems.

The default report is in a human readable text format. It is possible to instead request XML output with the -xml switch.

For scripting purposes, the -valonly and -lifonly switches are provided to restrict output to the actual pixel values, or the LocationInfo files identified for the pixel.

It is anticipated that additional reporting capabilities will be added to gdallocationinfo in the future.

Examples

Simple example reporting on pixel (256, 256) on the file utm.tif:

```
gdallocationinfo utm.tif 256 256
```

```
Report:
  Location: (256P,256L)
  Band 1:
    Value: 115
```

Query a VRT file providing the location in WGS84, and getting the result in XML:

```
gdallocationinfo -xml -wgs84 utm.vrt -117.5 33.75
```

```
<Report pixel="217" line="282">
  <BandReport band="1">
    <LocationInfo>
      <File>utm.tif</File>
    </LocationInfo>
    <Value>16</Value>
  </BandReport>
</Report>
```

21

gdalwarp

Syntax

```
gdalwarp [--help-general] [--formats]
    [-s_srs srs_def] [-t_srs srs_def] [-to "NAME=VALUE"]
    [-order n] [-tps] [-rpc] [-geoloc] [-et err_threshold]
    [-te xmin ymin xmax ymax] [-tr xres yres]
    [-tap] [-ts width height]
    [-wo "NAME=VALUE"] [-ot type] [-wt Byte/Int16]
    [-srcnodata "value [value...]"]
    [-dstnodata "value [value...]"] -dstalpha
    [-r resampling_method] [-wm memory_in_mb] [-multi] [-q]
    [-cutline datasource] [-cl layer] [-cwhere expression]
    [-csql statement] [-cblend dist_in_pixels]
    [-crop_to_cutline]
    [-of format] [-co "NAME=VALUE"]* [-overwrite]
    srcfile* dstfile
```

Description

The gdalwarp utility is an image mosaicking, reprojection and warp-ing utility. The program can reproject to any supported projection, and can also apply ground control points (GCPs) stored with the image if the image is "raw" with control information.

-s_srs srs def:
> Set source spatial reference. The coordinate systems that can be passed are anything supported by OGR which includes EPSG PCS and GCSes (i.e. EPSG:4296), PROJ.4 declarations (as above), or the name of a .prf file containing well known text.

-t_srs srs_def:
> Set target spatial reference. The coordinate systems that can be passed are anything supported by OGR (as above).

-to NAME=VALUE:
> Set a transformer option suitable to pass to the GDAL API call GDALCreateGenImgProjTransformer2().[76]

[76] See http://loc8.cc/gdal_projtrans

-order n:
> Order of polynomial used for warping (1 to 3). The default is to select a polynomial order based on the number of GCPs.

-tps:
> Force use of thin plate spline transformer based on available GCPs.

-rpc:
> Force use of RPCs.

-geoloc:
> Force use of Geolocation Arrays.

-et err_threshold:
> Error threshold for transformation approximation (in pixel units - defaults to 0.125).

-te xmin ymin xmax ymax:
> Set georeferenced extents of output file to be created (in target SRS).

-tr xres yres:
> Set output file resolution (in target georeferenced units). **Note that -tr cannot be used with -ts.**

-tap: [v1.8+]
> Target Aligned Pixels - align the coordinates of the extent of the

output file to the values of the -tr, such that the aligned extent includes the minimum extent.

-ts *width height:*
Set output file size in pixels and lines. If width or height is set to 0, the other dimension will be guessed from the computed resolution. **Note that -ts cannot be used with -tr.**

-wo *"NAME=VALUE":*
Set a warp option. The GDALWarpOptions::papszWarpOptions API docs[77] show all options. Multiple -wo options may be listed.

[77] http://loc8.cc/gdal_warpopt

-ot *type:*
Select the data type for the output bands: Byte, Int16, UInt16, UInt32 Int32, Float32, Float64, CInt16, CInt32, CFloat32, CFloat64.

-wt *type:*
Working pixel data type. The data type of pixels in the source image and destination image buffers.

-r *resampling_method:*
Resampling method to use. Available methods are:

near: Nearest neighbour resampling (default, fastest algorithm, worst interpolation quality)

bilinear: Bilinear resampling

cubic: Cubic resampling

cubicspline: Cubic spline resampling

lanczos: Lanczos windowed sinc resampling

-srcnodata *value [value...]:*
Set nodata masking values for input bands (different values can be supplied for each band). If more than one value is supplied all values should be quoted to keep them together as a single operating system argument. Masked values will not be used in interpolation. Use a value of None to ignore intrinsic nodata settings on the source dataset.

-dstnodata *value [value...]:*
Set nodata values for output bands (different values can be supplied for each band). If more than one value is supplied all values

should be quoted to keep them together as a single operating system argument. New files will be initialized to this value and if possible the nodata value will be recorded in the output file.

-dstalpha:
Create an output alpha band to identify nodata (unset/transparent) pixels.

-wm memory_in_mb:
Set the amount of memory (in megabytes) that the warp API is allowed to use for caching.

-multi:
Use multithreaded warping implementation. Multiple threads will be used to process chunks of image and perform input/output operation simultaneously.

-q:
Suppress progress monitor and other non-error output.

-of format:
Select the output format. The default is GeoTIFF (GTiff). Use the short format name.

-co "NAME=VALUE":
Passes a creation option to the output format driver. Multiple -co options may be listed. See format specific documentation for legal creation options for each format.

-cutline datasource:
Enable use of a blend cutline from the name OGR support datasource.

-cl layername:
Select the named layer from the cutline datasource.

-cwhere expression:
Restrict desired cutline features based on attribute query.

-csql query:
Select cutline features using an SQL query instead of from a layer with -cl.

-cblend distance:
Set a blend distance to use to blend over cutlines (in pixels).

EXAMPLE 209

-crop_to_cutline:
    Crop the extent of the target dataset to the extent of the cutline.

-overwrite: [v1.8+]
    Overwrite the target dataset if it already exists.

srcfile:
    The source file name(s).

dstfile:
    The destination file name.

Mosaicking into an existing output file is supported if the output file already exists. The spatial extent of the existing file will not be modified to accommodate new data, so you may have to remove it in that case.

Polygon cutlines may be used to restrict the area of the destination file that may be updated, including blending. If the OGR layer containing the cutline features has no explicit SRS, the cutline features must be in the georeferenced units of the destination file.

Example

Warp an eight bit "SPOT" satellite scene stored in GeoTIFF, with control points, mapping the corners from lat/long into a UTM projection:

```
gdalwarp -t_srs '+proj=utm +zone=11 +datum=WGS84' \
        raw_spot.tif utm11.tif
```

Warp the second channel of an ASTER image stored in HDF that has control points mapping the corners to lat/long, into a UTM projection:

```
gdalwarp -t_srs '+proj=utm +zone=11 +dataum=WGS84' \
        HDF4_SDS:ASTER_L1B:"pg-PR1B00-2002031402_100":2 \
        pg-PR1B00-2002031402_100_2.tif
```

Simplified specification of projection information can be provided using EPSG code numbers, for example to warp from a WGS84 system to projected UTM Zone 10, use the official EPSG code numbers 4326 and 26910[78]

```
gdalwarp -s_srs epsg:4326 -t_srs epsg:26910 \
             input.tif output.tif
```

[78] Find EPSG codes: http://loc8.cc/srs

22

gdal_polygonize.py

PRODUCES A POLYGON FEATURE LAYER FROM A RASTER

> **Tip**
> This is a Python script, and will only work if GDAL was built
> with Python support.

Syntax

```
gdal_polygonize.py [-8] [-nomask] [-mask filename]
                   raster_file [-b band]
                   [-q] [-f ogr_format]
                   out_file [layer] [fieldname]
```

Description

This utility creates vector polygons for all connected regions of pixels in the raster sharing a common pixel value. Each polygon is
created with an attribute indicating the pixel value of that polygon.
A raster mask may also be provided to determine which pixels are
eligible for processing.

The utility will create the output vector datasource if it does not
already exist. By default the GML format is used as the output.

The utility is based on the GDALPolygonize()[79] function which has additional details on the algorithm.

-8: [v1.10+]
Use 8 connectedness. Default is 4 connectedness.

-nomask:
Do not use the default validity mask for the input band (such as nodata, or alpha masks).

-mask filename:
Use the first band of the specified file as a validity mask (zero is invalid, non-zero is valid).

raster_file:
The source raster file from which polygons are derived.

-b band:
The band in raster_file to build the polygons from.

-f ogr_format:
Select the output format of the file to be created. Default is GML.

out_file:
The destination vector file to which the polygons will be written.

layer:
The name of the layer created to hold the polygon features.

fieldname:
The name of the field to create. Default in DN.

-q:
The script runs in quiet mode. The progress monitor is suppressed and routine messages are not displayed.

23

gdal_proximity.py

> **Tip**
>
> This is a Python script, and will only work if GDAL was built with Python support.

Syntax

```
gdal_proximity.py srcfile dstfile [-srcband n] [-dstband n]
                  [-of format] [-co name=value]*
                  [-ot type]
                  [-values n,n,n] [-distunits PIXEL/GEO]
                  [-maxdist n] [-nodata n] [-fixed-buf-val n]
```

Description

The `gdal_proximity.py` script generates a raster proximity map indicating the distance from the center of each pixel to the center of the nearest pixel identified as a target pixel. Target pixels are those in the source raster for which the raster pixel value is in the set of target pixel values.

srcfile:
   The source raster file used to identify target pixels.

dstfile:

The destination raster file to which the proximity map will be written. It may be a pre-existing file of the same size as `srcfile`. If it does not exist it will be created.

-srcband n:

Identifies the band in the source file to use (default is 1).

-dstband n:

Identifies the band in the destination file to use (default is 1).

-of format:

Select the output format. The default is GeoTIFF (GTiff). Use the short format name.[80]

[80] See the Raster Data Formats section on page 331 for a list of formats.

-co "NAME=VALUE":

Passes a creation option to the output format driver. Multiple `-co` options may be listed. See format specific documentation for legal creation options for each format.

-ot type:

Select the data type for the output bands: Byte, Int16, UInt16, UInt32 Int32, Float32, Float64, CInt16, CInt32, CFloat32, CFloat64.

-values n,n,n:

A list of target pixel values in the source image to be considered target pixels. If not specified, all non-zero pixels will be considered target pixels.

-distunits PIXEL/GEO:

Indicate whether distances generated should be in pixel or georeferenced coordinates (default `PIXEL`).

-maxdist n:

The maximum distance to be generated. All pixels beyond this distance will be assigned either the nodata value, or 65535. Distance is interpreted in pixels unless `-distunits GEO` is specified.

-nodata n:

Specify a nodata value to use for the destination proximity raster.

-fixed-buf-val n:

Specify a value to be applied to all pixels that are within the

`-maxdist` of target pixels (including the target pixels) instead of a distance value.

24

gdal_fillnodata.py

FILL RASTER REGIONS BY INTERPOLATION FROM EDGES

> **Tip**
>
> This is a Python script, and will only work if GDAL was built
> with Python support.

Syntax

```
gdal_fillnodata.py [-q] [-md max_distance]
                   [-si smooth_iterations]
                   [-o name=value] [-b band]
                   srcfile [-nomask] [-mask filename]
                   [-of format] [dstfile]
```

Description

The `gdal_fillnodata.py` script fills selection regions (usually nodata areas) by interpolating from valid pixels around the edges of
the area.

Additional details on the algorithm are available in the `GDALFillNodata()`
docs.[81]

[81] http://loc8.cc/gdal_fillno

-q:
   The script runs in quiet mode. The progress monitor is suppressed

and routine messages are not displayed.

-md *max_distance:*

The maximum distance (in pixels) that the algorithm will search out for values to interpolate.

-si *smooth_iterations:*

The number of 3x3 average filter smoothing iterations to run after the interpolation to dampen artifacts. The default is zero smoothing iterations.

-o *name=value:*

Specify a special argument to the algorithm. Currently none are supported.

-b *band:*

The band to operate on. Default is band 1.

srcfile:

The source raster file used to identify target pixels. Only one band is used.

-nomask:

Do not use the default validity mask for the input band (such as nodata, or alpha masks).

-mask *filename:*

Use the first band of the specified file as a validity mask (zero is invalid, non-zero is valid).

dstfile:

The new file to create with the interpolated result. If not provided, the source band is updated in place.

-of *format:*

Select the output format. The default is GeoTIFF (GTiff). Use the short format name.

25

gdalmove.py

> **Tip**
>
> This is a Python script, and will only work if GDAL was built with Python support.

Syntax

```
gdalmove.py [-s_srs <srs_defn>] -t_srs <srs_defn>
            [-et <max_pixel_err>] target_file
```

Description

Available from [**v1.10+**].

The gdalmove.py script transforms the bounds of a raster file from one coordinate system to another, and then updates the coordinate system and geotransform of the file. This is done without altering pixel values at all. It is loosely similar to using gdalwarp to transform an image but avoids the resampling step in order to prevent image damage. It is generally only suitable for transformations that are effectively linear in the area of the file.

If no error threshold value (-et) is provided then the file is not actually updated, but the errors that would be incurred are reported. If -et is provided then the file is only modified if the apparent error being introduced is less than the indicated threshold (in pixels).

Currently the transformed geotransform is computed based on the transformation of the top left, top right, and bottom left corners. A reduced overall error could be produced using a least squares fit of at least all four corner points.

-s_srs srs_defn:
Override the coordinate system of the file with the indicated coordinate system definition. Optional. If not provided the source coordinate system is read from the source file.

-t_srs srs_defn:
Defines the target coordinate system. This coordinate system will be written to the file after an update.

-et max_pixel_err:
The error threshold (in pixels) beyond which the file will not be updated. If not provided no update will be applied to the file, but errors will be reported.

target_file:
The file to be operated on. To update this must be a file format that supports in-place updates of the geotransform and SRS.[82]

[82] gdalinfo --formats denotes formats supporting in-place updates marked with rw+ next to the format name. e.g. NITF (rw+v)...

26

gdalmanage

Identify, delete, rename and copy raster data files

Syntax

```
gdalmanage mode [-r] [-u] [-f format]
           datasetname [newdatasetname]
```

The gdalmanage program can perform various operations on raster data files, depending on the chosen *mode.* This includes identifying raster data type and deleting, renaming or copying the files.

mode:
  Mode of operation:

  identify: List data type of file

  delete: Delete raster file

  rename: Change the name of the raster file

  copy: Create a copy of the raster file with a new name

-r:
  Recursively scan files/folders for raster files.

-u:
  Report failures if file type is unidentified.

-f format:

> Specify format of raster file if unknown by the application. Uses short data format name (e.g. *GTiff*).

newdatasetname:

> For copy and rename modes, you provide an *oldname* and a *newname* parameter, just like copy and move commands in an operating system.

Examples

Using identify mode

Report the data format of the raster file by using the *identify* mode and specifying a data file name:

```
gdalmanage identify NE1_50M_SR_W.tif
```

```
NE1_50M_SR_W.tif: GTiff
```

Recursive mode will scan subfolders and report the data format:

```
gdalmanage identify -r 50m_raster/
```

```
NE1_50M_SR_W/ne1_50m.jpg: JPEG
NE1_50M_SR_W/ne1_50m.png: PNG
NE1_50M_SR_W/ne1_50m_20pct.tif: GTiff
NE1_50M_SR_W/ne1_50m_band1.tif: GTiff
NE1_50M_SR_W/ne1_50m_print.png: PNG
NE1_50M_SR_W/NE1_50M_SR_W.aux: HFA
NE1_50M_SR_W/NE1_50M_SR_W.tif: GTiff
NE1_50M_SR_W/ne1_50m_sub.tif: GTiff
NE1_50M_SR_W/ne1_50m_sub2.tif: GTiff
```

Using copy mode

Copy the raster data file:

```
gdalmanage copy NE1_50M_SR_W.tif ne1_copy.tif
```

Using rename mode

Rename raster data file:

```
gdalmanage rename NE1_50M_SR_W.tif ne1_rename.tif
```

Using delete mode

Delete the raster data file:

```
gdalmanage delete NE1_50M_SR_W.tif
```

Part IV

OGR Vector Utilities

Table of Contents

1

OGR Utilities Overview

"The OGR Simple Features Library is a C++ open source library (and command line tools) providing read (and sometimes write) access to a variety of vector file formats including ESRI Shapefiles, S-57, SDTS, PostGIS, Oracle Spatial, and Mapinfo mid/mif and TAB formats" ... and more.[83]

[83] From http://gdal.org/ogr

OGR is part of the GDAL/OGR project, including both tools and programming libraries, with a focus on vector data access and processing. Though there are fewer command line tools than GDAL, they are still comprehensive for the purposes of conversion and reporting.[84]

[84] These tools can be further extended by writing your own programs in C++, Python, Java, and more, which can also link to geoprocessing libraries.

The following utilities are distributed as part of the OGR toolkit:

ogrinfo:
: Lists information about vector data sources

ogr2ogr:
: Converts vector data between formats

ogrtindex:
: Creates a MapServer tileindex

The `ogrinfo` utility is roughly equivalent to `gdalinfo` and `ogr2ogr` is a translation tool similar to `gdal_translate`; the difference being, OGR works with vector datasources and their internal layers as opposed to raster files and bands.

The other main OGR utility is `ogrtindex`, which is a convenient way to catalogue many vector datasets into a single file. This is used specifically for the OSGeo MapServer web mapping platform, but is also generally useful for catalogue purposes.

2

ogrinfo

Syntax

```
ogrinfo [--help-general] [-ro] [-q]
        [-where restricted_where]
        [-spat xmin ymin xmax ymax] [-fid fid]
        [-sql statement] [-dialect dialect]
        [-al] [-so] [-fields={YES/NO}]
        [-geom={YES/NO/SUMMARY}]
        [--formats]
        datasource_name [layer [layer ...]]
```

The `ogrinfo` program lists various information about an OGR supported data source to stdout (the terminal or command prompt).

-ro:
  Open the data source in read-only mode. Skips check for read/write ability.

-al:
  List all features of all layers (used instead of having to give layer names as arguments).

-so:
  Summary Only: suppress listing of features, show only the sum-

mary information like projection, schema, feature count and extents.

-q:

Silence (quiet) verbose reporting of various information, including coordinate system, layer schema, extents, and feature count. Suppresses messages and INFO statements.

-where restricted_where:

An attribute query in the form of SQL WHERE statements. Only features matching the attribute query will be reported.

-sql statement:

Execute the indicated SQL statement and return the result.

-dialect dialect:

SQL dialect. In some cases can be used to use (unoptimized) OGR SQL instead of the native SQL of an RDBMS by passing OGRSQL. Starting with GDAL 1.10, the "SQLITE" dialect can also be used with any datasource.

-spat xmin ymin xmax ymax:

Set the area of interest. Only features within the rectangle will be reported. Features that have any portion within the rectangle will be reported. Features are not physically *clipped* to the area.

-fid fid:

If provided, only the feature with this feature id will be reported. Operates exclusive of the spatial or attribute queries.

To select several features based on their feature id, use the special fid field an OGR SQL statement, like: '-where "fid in (1,3,5)"'.

-fields ={YES/NO}: [v1.6+]

If set to NO the feature dump will not display field values. Default value is YES.

-geom ={YES/NO/SUMMARY}: [v1.6+]

If set to NO, the feature dump will not display the geometry. If set to SUMMARY, only a summary of the geometry will be displayed. If set to YES, the geometry will be reported in full OGC WKT format. Default value is YES.

--formats:
List the format drivers that are enabled.

datasource_name:
The data source to open. May be a filename, directory or other virtual name. See the OGR Vector Data Formats list for supported datasources.

layer:
One or more layer names may be reported.

If no layer names are passed, ogrinfo will report a list of available layers (and their layer-wide geometry type). If layer name(s) are given, their extents, coordinate system, feature count, geometry type, schema, and all features matching query parameters will be reported to the terminal. If no query parameters are provided, all features are reported.

Geometries are reported in OGC WKT format.

Examples

Report all layers in an NTF file:

```
ogrinfo wrk/SHETLAND_ISLANDS.NTF
```

```
INFO: Open of `wrk/SHETLAND_ISLANDS.NTF'
using driver `UK .NTF' successful.
1: BL2000_LINK (Line String)
2: BL2000_POLY (None)
3: BL2000_COLLECTIONS (None)
4: FEATURE_CLASSES (None)
```

This report shows four layers that are part of the NTF file. To see more details about a specific layer, provide its name as a second argument:

```
ogrinfo wrk/SHETLAND_ISLANDS.NT BL2000_LINK
```

The above provides verbose output for all the features in that layer. Use an attribute query (-where clause) to restrict the output of the features in a layer:

```
ogrinfo -ro -where 'GLOBAL_LINK_ID=185878' \
        wrk/SHETLAND_ISLANDS.NTF BL2000_LINK

INFO: Open of `wrk/SHETLAND_ISLANDS.NTF'
using driver `UK .NTF' successful.

Layer name: BL2000_LINK
Geometry: Line String
Feature Count: 1
Extent: (419794, 1069031) - (419927, 1069153)
Layer SRS WKT:
PROJCS["OSGB 1936 / British National Grid",
    GEOGCS["OSGB 1936",
        DATUM["OSGB_1936",
            SPHEROID["Airy 1830",6377563.396,299.3249646]],
        PRIMEM["Greenwich",0],
        UNIT["degree",0.0174532925199433]],
    PROJECTION["Transverse_Mercator"],
    PARAMETER["latitude_of_origin",49],
    PARAMETER["central_meridian",-2],
    PARAMETER["scale_factor",0.999601272],
    PARAMETER["false_easting",400000],
    PARAMETER["false_northing",-100000],
    UNIT["metre",1]]
LINE_ID: Integer (6.0)
GEOM_ID: Integer (6.0)
FEAT_CODE: String (4.0)
GLOBAL_LINK_ID: Integer (10.0)
TILE_REF: String (10.0)
OGRFeature(BL2000_LINK):2
  LINE_ID (Integer) = 2
  GEOM_ID (Integer) = 2
  FEAT_CODE (String) = (null)
  GLOBAL_LINK_ID (Integer) = 185878
  TILE_REF (String) = SHETLAND I
  LINESTRING (419832.100 1069046.300,419820.100 1069043.800,
  419805.100 1069046.000,419805.000 1069040.600,419809.400
```

3

ogr2ogr

CONVERTS VECTOR DATA BETWEEN FORMATS

> **Tips**
>
> The order of input and output datasources is different than
> gdal_translate. The destination datasource is provided first
> and the input(s) are second.

Syntax

```
ogr2ogr [--help-general] [-skipfailures]
        [-append] [-update]
        [-select field_list]
        [-where restricted_where]
        [-progress] [-sql <sql statement>]
        [-dialect dialect]
        [-preserve_fid] [-fid FID]
        [-spat xmin ymin xmax ymax]
        [-a_srs srs_def] [-t_srs srs_def]
        [-s_srs srs_def]
        [-f format_name] [-overwrite]
        [[-dsco NAME=VALUE] ...]


        dst_datasource_name src_datasource_name
```

```
                    [-lco NAME=VALUE] [-nln name] [-nlt type]
                    [layer [layer ...]]
```

Advanced Options

```
[-gt n]
[-clipsrc [xmin ymin xmax ymax]|WKT|datasource|spat_extent]
[-clipsrcsql sql_statement] [-clipsrclayer layer]
[-clipsrcwhere expression]
[-clipdst [xmin ymin xmax ymax]|WKT|datasource]
[-clipdstsql sql_statement] [-clipdstlayer layer]
[-clipdstwhere expression]
[-wrapdateline]
[[-simplify tolerance | [-segmentize max_dist] ]
[-fieldTypeToString All|(type1[,type2]*)]
[-splitlistfields] [-maxsubfields val]
[-explodecollections] [-zfield field_name]
[-gcp pixel line easting northing [elevation]]*
[-order n | -tps]
```

Description

This program can be used to convert vector data between both file and database formats, performing various operations during the process such as spatial or attribute selections, reducing the set of attributes, setting the output coordinate system, or even reprojecting the features during translation.

-f format_name:
Output data format name (default is *ESRI Shapefile*), some possible values are:

```
-f "ESRI Shapefile"
-f "TIGER"
-f "MapInfo File"
-f "GML"
-f "PostgreSQL"
-f "Ingres"
-f "KML"
```

Refer to the Vector Data Formats list of vector formats in the appendix for valid formats. Use the general `--formats` option to list formats supported by `ogr2ogr`.

-append:

Append to existing layer instead of creating new.

-overwrite:

Delete the output layer and recreate it empty.

-update:

Open existing output datasource in update mode rather than trying to create a new one.

-select field_list:

Comma-delimited list of fields from input layer to copy to the new layer. A field is skipped if mentioned previously in the list even if the input layer has duplicate field names. (Defaults to all; any field is skipped if a subsequent field with same name is found.)

-progress: [v1.7+]

Display progress on terminal. Only works if input layers have the "fast feature count" capability.

-sql sql_statement:

SQL statement to execute. The resulting table/layer will be saved to the output.

-dialect dialect:

SQL dialect. In some cases can be used to use (unoptimized) OGR SQL instead of the native SQL of an RDBMS by passing OGRSQL.

-where restricted_where:

Attribute query (like SQL WHERE).

-skipfailures:

Continue after a failure, skipping the failed feature.

-spat xmin ymin xmax ymax:

Spatial query extents. Only features whose geometry intersects the extents will be selected. The geometries will not be clipped unless -clipsrc is specified.

-dsco NAME=VALUE:

Dataset creation option (format specific).

-lco NAME=VALUE:
> Layer creation option (format specific).

-nln name:
> Assign an alternate name to the new layer.

-nlt type:
> Define the geometry type for the created layer. One of NONE, GEOMETRY, POINT, LINESTRING, POLYGON, GEOMETRYCOLLECTION, MULTIPOINT, MULTIPOLYGON, or MULTILINESTRING. Add 25D to the name to get 2.5D versions.

-a_srs srs_def:
> Assign an output SRS. See sidebar for more on srs_def.[85]

[85] srs_def can be a full WKT definition (hard to escape properly), or a well known definition (i.e. EPSG:4326) or a file with a WKT definition.

-t_srs srs_def:
> Reproject/transform to this SRS on output. See sidebar for more on srs_def.

-s_srs srs_def:
> Override source SRS. See sidebar for more on srs_def.

-fid fid:
> If provided, only the feature with this feature id will be reported. Operates exclusive of the spatial or attribute queries. Note: if you want to select several features based on their feature id, you can also use the fact the 'fid' is a special field recognized by OGR SQL. So:

```
-where "fid in (1,3,5)"
```

> would select features 1, 3 and 5.

Advanced Option Details

-gt n:
> Group n features per transaction (default 200). For some datasources increasing this number can improve performance as more transactions can be made during a single connection to the target datasource. Availability of this operation depends on the datasource driver supporting it.

-clipsrc [xmin ymin xmax ymax] | WKT | datasource | spat_extent: [v1.7+]
> Clip geometries to the specified bounding box (expressed in source

SRS), WKT geometry (POLYGON or MULTIPOLYGON), from a data-source or to the spatial extent of the -spat option if you use the spat_extent keyword. When specifying a datasource, you will generally want to use it in combination of the -clipsrclayer, -clipsrcwhere or -clipsrcsql options.

-clipsrcsql sql_statement:
Select desired geometries using an SQL query instead.

-clipsrclayer layername:
Select the named layer from the source clip datasource.

-clipsrcwhere expression:
Restrict desired geometries based on attribute query.

-clipdst xmin ymin xmax ymax: [v1.7+]
Clip geometries after reprojection to the specified bounding box (expressed in dest SRS), WKT geometry (POLYGON or MULTIPOLYGON) or from a datasource. When specifying a datasource, you will generally want to use it in combination of the -clipdstlayer, -clipdstwhere or -clipdstsql options.

-clipdstsql sql_statement:
Select desired geometries using an SQL query instead.

-clipdstlayer layername:
Select the named layer from the destination clip datasource.

-clipdstwhere expression:
Restrict desired geometries based on attribute query.

-wrapdateline: [v1.7+]
Split geometries crossing the dateline meridian (long. = +/- 180deg).

-simplify: [v1.9+]
Distance tolerance for simplification. This method will preserve topology, in particular for polygon geometries.

-segmentize max_dist: [v1.6+]
Maximum distance between two nodes. Used to create intermediate points.

-fieldTypeToString type1, ...: [v1.7+]
Converts any field of the specified type to a field of type string in

the destination layer. Valid types are: Integer, Real, String, Date, Time, DateTime, Binary, IntegerList, RealList, StringList.

Special value All can be used to convert all fields to strings. This is an alternate way to using the CAST operator of OGR SQL, that may avoid typing a long SQL query.

-splitlistfields: [v1.8+]
Split fields of type StringList, RealList or IntegerList into as many fields of type String, Real or Integer as necessary.

-maxsubfields val:
To be combined with -splitlistfields to limit the number of subfields created for each split field.

-explodecollections: [v1.8+]
Produce one feature for each geometry in any kind of geometry collection in the source file.

-zfield field_name: [v1.8+]
Uses the specified field to fill the Z coordinate of geometries.

-gcp ungeoref_x ungeoref_y georef_x georef_y elevation: [v1.10+]
Add the indicated ground control point. This option may be provided multiple times to provide a set of GCPs.

-order n: [v1.10+]
Order of polynomial used for warping (1 to 3). The default is to select a polynomial order based on the number of GCPs.

-tps: [v1.10+]
Force use of thin plate spline transformer based on available GCPs.

Examples

Convert an ESRI Shapefile into a GML file[86]

[86] More examples are given in the individual format pages on http://gdal.org.

```
ogr2ogr -f GML  output.gml input.shp
```

Use ogrinfo to list layers in a NOAA ENC S-57 file, then do a conversion (below):

```
ogrinfo US5NC54M.000
ERROR 4: S57 Driver doesn't support update.
Had to open data source read-only.
```

```
INFO: Open of `US5NC54M.000'
      using driver `S57' successful.
1: DSID (None)
2: AIRARE
3: BCNLAT (Point)
4: BCNSPP (Point)
8: BOYLAT (Point)
...
```

Convert only the BOYLAT layer from the above S-57 file, into a KML format file:

```
ogr2ogr -f KML output.kml US5NC54M.000 BOYLAT
```

Project a GML file from lat/long coordinates into a local UTM projection (UTM Zone 10 is EPSG:26910), by defining the source (-s_srs) and target (-t_srs) coordinate systems. If the source system is already defined in the data, then you can leave off -s_srs:

```
ogr2ogr -f GML -s_srs EPSG:4326 -t_srs EPSG:26910 \
        output.gml input.gml
```

Append to and update an existing layer (both flags need to be used), while converting from a .tab file to PostgreSQL database:

```
ogr2ogr -update -append -f PostgreSQL PG:dbname=warmerda abc.tab
```

Reproject a shapefile to EPSG:4326 while clipping to a bounding box (-5,40,15,55); the source projection was already defined in the data:

```
ogr2ogr -wrapdateline -t_srs EPSG:4326 \
        -clipdst -5 40 15 55 \
        france_4326.shp europe_laea.shp
```

4

ogrtindex

CREATES A MAPSERVER TILEINDEX

Syntax

```
ogrtindex [-lnum n]... [-lname name]... [-f output_format]
          [-write_absolute_path] [-skip_different_projection]
          output_dataset src_dataset...
```

Description

The ogrtindex program can be used to create a *tileindex*—a file containing a list of the identities of a collection of data files along with their spatial extents. These are primarily intended to be used with MapServer[87] for tiled access to layers using the OGR connection type.

[87] http://mapserver.org

The following options apply:

-lnum n:
    Add layer number n from each source file in the tile index.

-lname name:
    Add the layer named name from each source file in the tile index.

-f output_format:
    Select an output format name. The default is to create a shape-

file. For a list of format name options, see the Vector Data Formats section on page 337, or run ogr2ogr --formats to list what is available to the ogrtindex command on your system.

-tileindex field_name:
> The name to use for the dataset name. Defaults to LOCATION.

-write_absolute_path:
> Filenames are written with absolute paths.

-skip_different_projection:
> Only layers with the same projection settings as layers already inserted in the tileindex will be inserted.

If no -lnum or -lname arguments are given it is assumed that all layers in source datasets should be added to the tile index as independent records.

If the tile index already exists it will be appended to, otherwise it will be created.

NOTE: No attempt is made to copy the coordinate system definition from the source datasets to the tile index (as is expected by MapServer when PROJECTION AUTO is in use).

Example

Create a shapefile (tindex.shp) containing a tile index of the layers in all the shapefiles in a directory:

```
ogrtindex tindex.shp *.shp
```

The results can then be easily viewed using ogrinfo:

```
ogrinfo tindex.shp tindex

INFO: Open of `tindex.shp'
      using driver `ESRI Shapefile' successful.

Layer name: tindex
Geometry: Polygon
Feature Count: 2
```

EXAMPLE 245

```
Extent: (-166.532482, -50.669625) - (176.093829, 81.955278)
Layer SRS WKT:
(unknown)
LOCATION: String (200.0)
OGRFeature(tindex):0
  LOCATION (String) = lakes1.shp,0
  POLYGON ((-165.965618939309223 -50.669624818377486,-165.96...


OGRFeature(tindex):1
  LOCATION (String) = lakes2.shp,0
  POLYGON ((-166.532482065659877 7.997570932184107,-166.5324...
```

Part V

PROJ.4 Projection Utilities

1

PROJ.4

Mathematically transforming map data from spherical lat/lon coordinates to a flat cartographic presentation requires the use of coordinate system projection utilities. While this area of science is deep and filled with fantastic equations and formulae, most digital cartographers have the benefit of several command line tools and programming libraries dedicated to this kind of heavy lifting.

This part of the book deals with the two primary tools provided by the PROJ.4 project.[88] These two command line utilities are called `proj` and `cs2cs`. See the next two chapters for more about their usage.

[88] PROJ.4 website: `http://loc8.cc/proj`

A comprehensive set of details is also available in Appendix 1 - Projection Library Options on page 319. This shows the variety of projection related options that may be used not only by these two commands but also by the broader GDAL/OGR toolset—anywhere that projections are used.

For a more detailed, yet gentle, introduction to projections, see *The Geospatial Desktop*—a full featured book about open source desktop GIS. Here is an excerpt:

> If the world were flat, it would be a lot easier---at least on mapmakers.

Unfortunately, that's not the case, so we're faced with the age-old problem of depicting features on a spheroid (that's the earth) on a flat piece of paper (or screen).

To solve this problem over the years, people have come up with the concept of map projections. The key thing to remember about projections is that none of them is perfect. You simply can't represent the entire earth (or even a small part of it) on a flat surface without some distortion. The amount of distortion varies with the projection. Many projections are quite good when used for a small or regional area. If you try to use the same projection for a larger area, the distortion increases.

—Gary Sherman, *The Geospatial Desktop* (Locate Press, 2012)
http://locatepress.com/gsd

2

proj

There are two `proj` related user utility commands for projecting coordinates:

proj: Forward cartographic projection filter

invproj: Inverse cartographic projection filter

Both commands have the same set of options:

```
proj | invproj [ -beEfiIlormsStTvVwW [args] ]
                [ +opts[=arg] ]
                [ files ]
```

Description

`proj` and `invproj` perform respective forward and inverse transformation of cartographic data to or from Cartesian data with a wide range of selectable projection functions.

The following control parameters can appear in any order:

-b:
Special option for binary coordinate data input and output through standard input and standard output. Data is assumed to be in system type *double* floating point words. This option is to be used when `proj` is a *son* process and allows bypassing formatting operations.

-i:

Selects binary input only (see -b option).

-I:

Alternate method to specify inverse projection. Redundant when used with invproj.

-o:

Selects binary output only (see -b option).

-t a:

A specifies a character employed as the first character to denote a control line to be passed through without processing. This option applicable to ASCII input only. (# is the default value).

-e string:

String is an arbitrary string to be output if an error is detected during data transformations. The default value is: \t. Note that if the -b, -i or -o options are employed, an error is returned as HUGE_VAL value for both return values.

-E:

Causes the input coordinates to be copied to the output line prior to printing the converted values.

-l[p|P|=|e|u|d]id:

List projection identifiers with -l, -lp or -lP (expanded) that can be selected with +proj. -l=id gives expanded description of projection *id*. List ellipsoid identifiers with -le, that can be selected with +ellps or -lu list of Cartesian to meter conversion factors that can be selected with +units.

-r:

This options reverses the order of the expected input from longitude-latitude or x-y to latitude-longitude or y-x.

-s:

This options reverses the order of the output from x-y or longitude-latitude to y-x or latitude-longitude.

-S:

Causes estimation of *meridional* and *parallel* scale factors, *area* scale factor and *angular distortion*, and *maximum* and *minimum* scale factors to be listed between <> for each input point. For conformal projections meridional and parallel scales factors will be equal and angular distortion zero. Equal area projections will have an area factor of 1.

-m mult:

The Cartesian data may be scaled by the *mult* parameter. When processing data in a forward projection mode the Cartesian output values are multiplied by *mult* otherwise the input Cartesian values are divided by *mult* before inverse projection. If the first two characters of *mult* are 1/ or 1: then the reciprocal value of *mult* is employed.

-f format:

Format is a *printf* format string to control the form of the output values. For inverse projections, the output will be in degrees when this option is employed. If a format is specified for inverse projection the output data will be in decimal degrees. The default format is %.2f for forward projection and DMS for inverse.

-[w | W] n:

N is the number of significant fractional digits to employ for seconds output (when the option is not specified, -w3 is assumed). When -W is employed the fields will be constant width and with leading zeros.

-v:

Causes a listing of cartographic control parameters tested for and used by the program to be printed prior to input data. Should not be used with the -T option.

-V:

This option causes an expanded annotated listing of the characteristics of the projected point. -v **is implied with this option**.

-T ulow,uhi,vlow,vhi,res[,umax,vmax]:

This option creates a set of bivariate Chebyshev polynomial coefficients that approximate the selected cartographic projection on *stdout*. The values *low* and *hi* denote the range of the input where the *u* or *v* prefixes apply to respective longitude-x or latitude-y depending upon whether a forward or inverse projection is selected.

Res is an integer number specifying the power of 10 precision of the approximation. For example, a *res* of -3 specifies an approximation with an accuracy better than .001. *Umax,* and *vmax* specify maximum degree of the polynomials (default: 15).

The +args run-line arguments are associated with cartographic parameters and usage varies with projection and for a complete description see *Cartographic Projection Procedures for the UNIX Environment—A User's Manual)* and supplementary documentation for Release 4.

Additional projection control parameters may be contained in two auxiliary control files: the first is optionally referenced with the +init=file:id and the second is always processed after the name of the projection has been established from either the run-line or the contents of +init file. The environment parameter PROJ_LIB establishes the default directory for a file reference without an absolute path.

One or more *files* (processed in left to right order) specify the source of data to be transformed. A - symbol will specify the location of processing standard input. If no files are specified, the input is assumed to be from *stdin.* For ASCII input data the two data values must be in the first two white space separated fields and when both input and output are ASCII all trailing portions of the input line are appended to the output line.

Input geographic data (longitude and latitude) must be in DMS format and input Cartesian data must be in units consistent with the ellipsoid major axis or sphere radius units. Output geographic coordinates will be in DMS (if the -w switch is not employed) and precise to 0.001" with trailing, zero-valued minute-second fields deleted.

Example

The following script will perform UTM forward projection with a standard UTM central meridian nearest longitude 112°W:

```
proj +proj=utm +lon_0=112w +ellps=clrk66 \
     -r <<EOF
45d15'33.1"     111.5W
45d15.551666667N     -111d30
+45.25919444444     111d30'000w
EOF
```

The geographic values of this example are equivalent and meant as examples of various forms of DMS input. The x-y output data will appear as three lines of:

```
460769.27     5011648.45
```

See Also

- *Cartographic Projection Procedures for the UNIX Environment—A User's Manual,* (Evenden, 1990, Open-file report 90–284).
- *Map Projections Used by the U. S. Geological Survey* (Snyder, 1984, USGS Bulletin 1532).
- *Map Projections—A Working Manual* (Synder, 1988, USGS Prof. Paper 1395).
- *An Album of Map Projections* (Snyder & Voxland, 1989, USGS Prof. Paper 1453).

Home page

http://proj.osgeo.org

3

cs2cs

cs2cs - cartographic coordinate system filter

Syntax

```
cs2cs [ -eEfIlrstvwW [args] ]
      [ +opts[=arg] ]
      [+to [+opts[=arg]]
      [ files ]
```

Description

cs2cs performs transformation between the source and destination cartographic coordinate system on a set of input points. The coordinate system transformation can include translation between projected and geographic coordinates as well as the application of datum shifts.

The following control parameters can appear in any order:

-I:

Method to specify inverse translation, convert from +to coordinate system to the primary coordinate system defined.

-t a:

A specifies a character employed as the first character to denote a control line to be passed through without processing. This option applicable to ASCII input only. (# is the default value).

-e string:

String is an arbitrary string to be output if an error is detected during data transformations. The default value is: \t. Note that if the -b, -i, or -o options are employed, an error is returned as HUGE_VAL value for both return values.

-E:

Causes the input coordinates to be copied to the output line prior to printing the converted values.

-l[p | P | = | e | u | d]id:

List projection identifiers with -l, -lp or -lP (expanded) that can be selected with +proj. -l=id gives expanded description of projection *id.* List ellipsoid identifiers with -le, that can be selected with +ellps, -lu list of Cartesian to meter conversion factors that can be selected with +units or -ld list of datums that can be selected with +datum.

-r:

This options reverses the order of the expected input from longitude-latitude or x-y to latitude-longitude or y-x.

-s:

This options reverses the order of the output from x-y or longitude-latitude to y-x or latitude-longitude.

-f format:

Format is a *printf* format string to control the form of the output values. For inverse projections, the output will be in degrees when this option is employed. If a format is specified for inverse projection the output data will be in decimal degrees. The default format is %.2f for forward projection and DMS for inverse.

-[w | W]n:

n is the number of significant fractional digits to employ for seconds output (when the option is not specified, -w3 is assumed). When -W is employed the fields will be constant width and with leading zeros.

-v:

    Causes a listing of cartographic control parameters tested for and used by the program to be printed prior to input data.

The +args run-line arguments are associated with cartographic parameters and usage varies with projection and for a complete description see *Cartographic Projection Procedures for the UNIX Environment—A User's Manual)* and supplementary documentation for Release 4.

The cs2cs program requires two coordinate system definitions. The first (or primary is defined based on all projection parameters not appearing after the +to argument. All projection parameters appearing after the +to argument are considered the definition of the second coordinate system. If there is no second coordinate system defined, a geographic coordinate system based on the datum and ellipsoid of the source coordinate system is assumed. Note that the source and destination coordinate system can both be projections, both be geographic, or one of each and may have the same or different datums.

Additional projection control parameters may be contained in two auxiliary control files: the first is optionally referenced with the +init=file:id and the second is always processed after the name of the projection has been established from either the run-line or the contents of +init file. The environment parameter PROJ_LIB establishes the default directory for a file reference without an absolute path. This is also used for supporting files like datum shift files.

One or more *files* (processed in left to right order) specify the source of data to be transformed. A - symbol will specify the location of processing standard input. If no files are specified, the input is assumed to be from *stdin.* For input data the two data values must be in the first two white space separated fields and when both input and output are ASCII all trailing portions of the input line are appended to the output line.

Input geographic data (longitude and latitude) must be in DMS format and input Cartesian data must be in units consistent with the ellipsoid major axis or sphere radius units. Output geographic coordinates will be in DMS (if the -w switch is not employed) and precise to 0.001" with trailing, zero-valued minute-second fields deleted.

Example

The following script will transform the input NAD83 geographic coordinates into NAD27 coordinates in the UTM projection with zone 10 selected:

```
cs2cs +proj=latlong +datum=NAD83
        +to +proj=utm +zone=10 +datum=NAD27 -r <<EOF
45d15'33.1"     111.5W
45d15.551666667N        -111d30
+45.25919444444         111d30'000w
EOF
```

The geographic values of this example are equivalent and meant as examples of various forms of DMS input. The x-y output data will appear as three lines of:

```
1402285.99     5076292.42 0.000
```

Example converting DMS to/from DD

Input coordinates can come from the command line or an external file. Assuming a file containing DMS (degree, minute, seconds) style, looks like:

```
124d10'20"W     52d14'22"N
122d20'05"W     54d12'00"N
```

Use the cs2cs command, specifying how the print format will be returned, using the -f option. In this case -f "%.6f" explicitly requesting a decimal degree number with 6 decimals:

```
cs2cs -f "%.6f" +proj=latlong +datum=WGS84 input.txt
```

Will return the results, notice no 3D/Z value was provided, so none is returned:

```
-124.172222    52.239444 0.000000
-122.334722    54.200000 0.000000
```

To do the inverse, remove the formatting option and provide a list of values in decimal degree (DD):

```
cs2cs +proj=latlong +datum=WGS84 inputdms.txt

124d10'19.999"W    52d14'21.998"N 0.000
122d20'4.999"W     54d12'N 0.000
```

4

gdalsrsinfo

LISTS SRS INFO IN A NUMBER OF FORMATS (WKT, PROJ.4, ETC.)

Syntax

```
gdalsrsinfo [--help-general] [-h]
            [-p] [-V] [-o out_type]
            srs_def
```

Description

Available since **[v1.9+]**.

The gdalsrsinfo utility reports information about a given SRS from one of the following:

- The filename of a dataset supported by GDAL/OGR which contains SRS information
- Any of the usual GDAL/OGR forms (complete WKT, PROJ.4, EPSG:n or a file containing the SRS)

  srs_def:
  The filename of a dataset supported by GDAL/OGR from which to extract SRS information or text representing any of the usual GDAL/OGR forms (complete WKT, PROJ.4, EPSG:n) or a file containing the SRS in one of these forms.

--help-general -h:
  Show help and exit

-p:
  Pretty-print where applicable (e.g. WKT)

-V:
  Validate SRS

-o out_type:
  Output type { default, all, wkt_all, proj4, wkt, wkt_simple, wkt_noct, wkt_esri, mapinfo, xml }

Output types

- **default**: proj4 and wkt (default option)
- **all**: all options available
- **wkt_all**: all wkt options available
- **proj4**:PROJ.4 string
- **wkt**: OGC WKT format (full)
- **wkt_simple**: OGC WKT (simplified)
- **wkt_noct**: OGC WKT (without OGC CT params)
- **wkt_esri**: ESRI WKT format
- **mapinfo**: Mapinfo style CoordSys format
- **xml**: XML format (GML based)

Examples

Retrieve PROJ.4 and OGC WKT values from an EPSG code number:

```
gdalsrsinfo    "EPSG:4326"

PROJ.4 : '+proj=longlat +datum=WGS84 +no_defs '

OGC WKT :
GEOGCS["WGS 84",
    DATUM["WGS_1984",
        SPHEROID["WGS 84",6378137,298.257223563,
            AUTHORITY["EPSG","7030"]],
        AUTHORITY["EPSG","6326"]],
```

```
      PRIMEM["Greenwich",0,
          AUTHORITY["EPSG","8901"]],
      UNIT["degree",0.0174532925199433,
          AUTHORITY["EPSG","9122"]],
      AUTHORITY["EPSG","4326"]]
```

Retrieve PROJ.4 values from an ESRI .prj file:

```
gdalsrsinfo -o proj4 osr/data/lcc_esri.prj
```

```
'+proj=lcc +lat_1=34.33333333333334 +lat_2=36.16666666666666 \
 +lat_0=33.75 +lon_0=-79 +x_0=609601.22 +y_0=0 +datum=NAD83 \
 +units=m +no_defs '
```

Retrieve PROJ.4 values from a GeoTIFF file:

```
gdalsrsinfo -o proj4 landsat.tif
```

```
PROJ.4 : '+proj=utm +zone=19 +south +datum=WGS84 +units=m +no_defs '
```

Retrieve WKT projection definition from an EPSG number, with pretty print option:

```
$ gdalsrsinfo  -o wkt -p  "EPSG:32722"
```

```
PROJCS["WGS 84 / UTM zone 22S",
    GEOGCS["WGS 84",
        DATUM["WGS_1984",
            SPHEROID["WGS 84",6378137,298.257223563,
                AUTHORITY["EPSG","7030"]],
            AUTHORITY["EPSG","6326"]],
        PRIMEM["Greenwich",0,
            AUTHORITY["EPSG","8901"]],
        UNIT["degree",0.0174532925199433,
            AUTHORITY["EPSG","9122"]],
        AUTHORITY["EPSG","4326"]],
    PROJECTION["Transverse_Mercator"],
    PARAMETER["latitude_of_origin",0],
    PARAMETER["central_meridian",-51],
    PARAMETER["scale_factor",0.9996],
    PARAMETER["false_easting",500000],
```

```
            PARAMETER["false_northing",10000000],
            UNIT["metre",1,
                AUTHORITY["EPSG","9001"]],
            AXIS["Easting",EAST],
            AXIS["Northing",NORTH],
            AUTHORITY["EPSG","32722"]]
```

Retrieve projection definitions in all available formats from an EPSG number:

```
gdalsrsinfo  -o wkt_all  "EPSG:4618"

OGC WKT :
GEOGCS["SAD69",
    DATUM["South_American_Datum_1969",
        SPHEROID["GRS 1967 Modified",6378160,298.25,
            AUTHORITY["EPSG","7050"]],
        TOWGS84[-57,1,-41,0,0,0,0],
        AUTHORITY["EPSG","6618"]],
    PRIMEM["Greenwich",0,
        AUTHORITY["EPSG","8901"]],
    UNIT["degree",0.0174532925199433,
        AUTHORITY["EPSG","9122"]],
    AUTHORITY["EPSG","4618"]]

OGC WKT (simple) :
GEOGCS["SAD69",
    DATUM["South_American_Datum_1969",
        SPHEROID["GRS 1967 Modified",6378160,298.25],
        TOWGS84[-57,1,-41,0,0,0,0]],
    PRIMEM["Greenwich",0],
    UNIT["degree",0.0174532925199433]]

OGC WKT (no CT) :
GEOGCS["SAD69",
    DATUM["South_American_Datum_1969",
        SPHEROID["GRS 1967 Modified",6378160,298.25]],
    PRIMEM["Greenwich",0],
    UNIT["degree",0.0174532925199433]]
```

```
ESRI WKT :
GEOGCS["SAD69",
    DATUM["D_South_American_1969",
        SPHEROID["GRS_1967_Truncated",6378160,298.25]],
    PRIMEM["Greenwich",0],
    UNIT["Degree",0.017453292519943295]]
```

Part VI

OGR SQL

1

OGR SQL Statements & Functions

In this part of the book we present an overview of the various SQL based commands and functions that can be used throughout GDAL's OGR libraries and command line utilities.

Some references are made to the underlying programming libraries to help developers understand more directly how these apply behind the scenes.

For general OGR command users, don't let the more technical references scare you off! You can skip over some of the more technical references and look at the specific examples that are provided following the Overview section.

Overview

Behind the scenes, the `OGRDataSource` class supports executing commands against a datasource via the `OGRDataSource::ExecuteSQL()` method. While in theory any sort of command could be handled this way, in practise the mechanism is used to provide a subset of SQL SELECT capability to applications. This page discusses the generic SQL implementation implemented within OGR, and issues with driver specific SQL support.

Starting in GDAL/OGR 1.10, an alternate "dialect", the SQLite dialect, can be used instead of the OGRSQL dialect. Refer to the SQLite SQL dialect[89] documentation for more details.

[89] SQLite SQL dialect: http://gdal.org/ogr/ogr_sql_sqlite.html

The `OGRLayer` class also supports applying an attribute query filter to features returned using the `OGRLayer::SetAttributeFilter()` method. The syntax for the attribute filter is the same as the `WHERE` clause in the OGR SQL `SELECT` statement. So everything here with regard to the `WHERE` clause applies in the context of the `SetAttributeFilter()` method.

SELECT

The `SELECT` statement is used to fetch layer features (analogous to table rows in an database) with the result of the query represented as a temporary layer of features. The layers of the datasource are analogous to tables in an RDBMS and feature attributes are analogous to column values. The simplest form of OGR SQL SELECT statement looks like this:

```
SELECT * FROM polylayer
```

In this case all features are fetched from the layer named `polylayer`, and all attributes of those features are returned. This is essentially equivalent to accessing the layer directly. In this example the * is the list of fields to fetch from the layer, with * meaning that all fields should be fetched.

This slightly more sophisticated form still pulls all features from the layer but the schema will only contain the `EAS_ID` and `PROP_VALUE` attributes. Any other attributes would be discarded.

```
SELECT eas_id, prop_value FROM polylayer
```

A much more ambitious `SELECT`, restricting the features fetched with a `WHERE` clause, and sorting the results might look like:

```
SELECT * from polylayer
    WHERE prop_value > 220000.0 ORDER BY prop_value DESC
```

The following select statement will produce a table with just one feature, with one attribute (named something like count_eas_id) containing the number of distinct values of the eas_id attribute.

```
SELECT COUNT(DISTINCT eas_id) FROM polylayer
```

Field List Operators

The field list is a comma separate list of the fields to be carried into the output features from the source layer. They will appear on output features in the order they appear on in the field list, so the field list may be used to re-order the fields.

A special form of the field list uses the DISTINCT keyword. This returns a list of all the distinct values of the named attribute. When the DISTINCT keyword is used, only one attribute may appear in the field list. The DISTINCT keyword may be used against any type of field. Currently the distinctness test against a string value is case insensitive in OGR SQL. The result of a SELECT with a DISTINCT keyword is a layer with one column (named the same as the field operated on), and one feature per distinct value. Geometries are discarded. The distinct values are assembled in memory, so a lot of memory may be used for datasets with a large number of distinct values.

```
SELECT DISTINCT areacode FROM polylayer
```

There are also several summarization operators that may be applied to columns. When a summarization operator is applied to any field, then all fields must have summarization operators applied. The summarization operators are COUNT (a count of instances), AVG (numerical average), SUM (numerical sum), MIN (lexical or numerical minimum), and MAX (lexical or numerical maximum). This example produces a variety of summarization information on parcel property values:

```
SELECT MIN(prop_value), MAX(prop_value), AVG(prop_value), SUM(prop_value),
    COUNT(prop_value) FROM polylayer WHERE prov_name = "Ontario"
```

It is also possible to apply the COUNT() operator to a DISTINCT SELECT to get a count of distinct values, for instance:

```
SELECT COUNT(DISTINCT areacode) FROM polylayer
```

Prior to OGR 1.9.0, null values were counted in COUNT(column_name) or COUNT(DISTINCT column_name), which was not in accordance with the SQL standard. Starting in OGR 1.9.0, only non-null values are counted.

As a special case, the COUNT() operator can be given a * argument instead of a field name which is a short form for "count all the records."

```
SELECT COUNT(*) FROM polylayer
```

Field names can also be prefixed by a table name though this is only really meaningful when performing joins. It is further demonstrated in the JOIN section.

Field definitions can also be complex expressions using arithmetic, and functional operators. However, the DISTINCT keyword, and summarization operators like MIN, MAX, AVG and SUM may not be applied to expression fields.

```
SELECT cost+tax FROM invoice
```

or

```
SELECT CONCAT(owner_first_name,' ',owner_last_name)
FROM properties
```

Functions

Starting with OGR 1.8.2, the SUBSTR function can be used to extract a substring from a string using the syntax:

```
SUBSTR(string_expr, start_offset [, length])
```

It extracts a substring of string_expr, starting at offset start_offset (1 being the first character of string_expr, 2 the second one, etc...).

If `start_offset` is a negative value, the substring is extracted from the end of the string (-1 is the last character of the string, -2 the character before the last character, ...). If length is specified, up to length characters are extracted from the string. Otherwise the remainder of the string is extracted.

Note: for the time being, the character is considered to be equivalent to bytes, which may not be appropriate for multi-byte encodings like UTF-8.

```
SELECT SUBSTR('abcdef',1,2) FROM xxx    --> 'ab'
SELECT SUBSTR('abcdef',4)   FROM xxx    --> 'def'
SELECT SUBSTR('abcdef',-2)  FROM xxx    --> 'ef'
```

Using the field name alias

OGR SQL supports renaming the fields following the SQL92 specification by using the AS keyword according to the following example:

```
SELECT *, OGR_STYLE AS STYLE FROM polylayer
```

The field name alias can be used as the last operation in the column specification. Therefore we cannot rename the fields inside an operator, but we can rename the whole column expression, like these two:

```
SELECT COUNT(areacode) AS 'count' FROM polylayer
SELECT dollars/100.0 AS cents FROM polylayer
```

Changing the type of the fields

Starting with GDAL 1.6.0, OGR SQL supports changing the type of the columns by using the SQL92 compliant CAST operator according to the following example:

```
SELECT *, CAST(OGR_STYLE AS character(255)) FROM rivers
```

Casting to the following target types are supported:

1. character(field_length). By default, field_length=1.

2. float(field_length)

3. numeric(field_length, field_precision)

4. integer(field_length)

5. date(field_length)

6. time(field_length)

7. timestamp(field_length)

Specifying the `field_length` and/or the `field_precision` is optional. An explicit value of zero can be used as the width for `character()` to indicate variable width. Conversion to the 'integer list', 'double list' and 'string list' OGR data types are not supported, which doesn't conform to the SQL92 specification.

While the `CAST` operator can be applied anywhere in an expression, including a `WHERE` clause, the detailed control of output field format is only supported if the `CAST` operator is the "outer most" operator on a field in the field definition list. In other contexts it is still useful to convert between numeric, string, and date data types.

WHERE

The argument to the `WHERE` clause is a logical expression used to select records from the source layer. In addition to its use within the `WHERE` statement, the `WHERE` clause handling is also used for OGR attribute queries on regular layers via the `OGRLayer::SetAttributeFilter()` method.

In addition to the arithmetic and other functional operators available in expressions in the field selection clause of the `SELECT` statement, in the `WHERE` context, logical operators are also available and the evaluated value of the expression should be logical (true or false).

The available logical operators are =, !=, <>, <, >, <=, >=, `LIKE` and `ILIKE`, `BETWEEN` and `IN`. Most of the operators are self explanatory, but is is worth noting that != is the same as <>, the string equality is case insensitive, but the <, >, <= and >= operators *are* case sensitive. Both the LIKE and ILIKE operators are case insensitive.

The value argument to the LIKE operator is a pattern against which the value string is matched. In this pattern percent (%) matches any number of characters, and underscore (_) matches any one character. An optional ESCAPE escape_char clause can be added so that the percent or underscore characters can be searched as regular characters, by being preceded with the escape_char.

```
String          Pattern        Matches?
------          -------        --------
Alberta         ALB%           Yes
Alberta         _lberta        Yes
St. Alberta     _lberta        No
St. Alberta     %lberta        Yes
Robarts St.     %Robarts%      Yes
12345           123%45         Yes
123.45          12?45          No
N0N 1P0         %N0N%          Yes
L4C 5E2         %N0N%          No
```

The IN takes a list of values as its argument and tests the attribute value for membership in the provided set.

```
Value           Value Set              Matches?
------          -------                --------
321             IN (456,123)           No
"Ontario"       IN ("Ontario","BC")    Yes
"Ont"           IN ("Ontario","BC")    No
1               IN (0,2,4,6)           No
```

The syntax of the BETWEEN operator is field_name BETWEEN value1 AND value2 and it is equivalent to field_name >= value1 AND field_name <= value2.

In addition to the above binary operators, there are additional operators for testing if a field is null or not. These are the IS NULL and

IS NOT NULL operators.

Basic field tests can be combined in more complicated predicates using logical operators include AND, OR, and the unary logical NOT. Subexpressions should be bracketed to make precedence clear. Some more complicated predicates are:

```
SELECT * FROM poly WHERE (prop_value >= 100000) \
                   AND (prop_value < 200000)
SELECT * FROM poly WHERE NOT (area_code LIKE "N0N%")
SELECT * FROM poly WHERE (prop_value IS NOT NULL) \
                   AND (prop_value < 100000)
```

WHERE Limitations

1. Fields must all come from the primary table (the one listed in the FROM clause).

2. All string comparisons are case insensitive except for <, >, <= and >=.

ORDER BY

The ORDER BY clause is used to force the returned features to be reordered into sorted order (ascending or descending) on one of the field values. Ascending (increasing) order is the default if neither the ASC or DESC keyword is provided. For example:

```
SELECT * FROM property WHERE class_code = 7 \
                      ORDER BY prop_value DESC
SELECT * FROM property ORDER BY prop_value
SELECT * FROM property ORDER BY prop_value ASC
SELECT DISTINCT zip_code FROM property ORDER BY zip_code
```

Note that ORDER BY clauses cause two passes through the feature set. One to build an in-memory table of field values by feature id, and a second pass to fetch the features by feature id in the sorted order. For formats which cannot efficiently randomly read features by feature id, this can be a very expensive operation.

Sorting of string field values is case sensitive, rather than case insensitive like in most other parts of OGR SQL.

JOINs

OGR SQL supports a limited form of one-to-one JOIN. This allows records from a secondary table to be looked up based on a shared key between it and the primary table being queried. For instance, a table of city locations might include a nation_id column that can be used as a reference into a secondary nation table to fetch a nation name. A joined query might look like:

```
SELECT city.*, nation.name FROM city
    LEFT JOIN nation ON city.nation_id = nation.id
```

This query would result in a table with all the fields from the city table, and an additional nation.name field with the nation name pulled from the nation table by looking for the record in the nation table that has the id field with the same value as the city.nation_id field.

Joins introduce a number of additional issues. One is the concept of table qualifiers on field names. For instance, referring to city.nation_id instead of just nation_id to indicate the nation_id field from the city layer. The table name qualifiers may only be used in the field list, and within the ON clause of the join.

Wildcards are also somewhat more involved. All fields from the primary table (city in this case) and the secondary table (nation in this case) may be selected using the usual * wildcard. But the fields of just one of the primary or secondary table may be selected by prefixing the asterisk with the table name.

The field names in the resulting query layer will be qualified by the table name, if the table name is given as a qualifier in the field list. In addition field names will be qualified with a table name if they would conflict with earlier fields. For instance, the following select would return a result set with a name, nation_id, nation.nation_id and nation.name field if the city and nation tables both have the nation_id and name fieldnames.

```
SELECT * FROM city LEFT JOIN nation ON city.nation_id = nation.nation_id
```

On the other hand if the nation table had a continent_id field, but the city table did not, then that field would not need to be qualified in the result set. However, if the select statement looked like the following, all result fields would be qualified by the table name.

```
SELECT city.*, nation.* FROM city
     LEFT JOIN nation ON city.nation_id = nation.nation_id
```

In the above examples, the nation table was found in the same datasource as the city table. However, the OGR join support includes the ability to join against a table in a different data source, potentially of a different format. This is indicated by qualifying the secondary table name with a datasource name. In this case the secondary datasource is opened using normal OGR semantics and utilized to access the secondary table until the query result is no longer needed.

```
LEFT JOIN '/usr2/data/nation.dbf'.nation
   ON city.nation_id = nation.nation_id
```

While not necessarily very useful, it is also possible to introduce table aliases to simplify some SELECT statements. This can also be useful to disambiguate situations where tables of the same name are being used from different data sources. For instance, if the actual tables names were messy we might want to do something like:

```
SELECT c.name, n.name FROM project_615_city c
   LEFT JOIN '/usr2/data/project_615_nation.dbf'.project_615_nation n
          ON c.nation_id = n.nation_id
```

It is possible to do multiple joins in a single query.

```
SELECT city.name, prov.name, nation.name FROM city
```

```
LEFT JOIN province ON city.prov_id = province.id
LEFT JOIN nation ON city.nation_id = nation.id
```

JOIN Limitations

1. Joins can be very expensive operations if the secondary table is not indexed on the key field being used.

2. Joined fields may not be used in `WHERE` clauses, or `ORDER BY` clauses at this time. The join is essentially evaluated after all primary table subsetting is complete, and after the `ORDER BY` pass.

3. Joined fields may not be used as keys in later joins. So you could not use the province id in a city to lookup the province record, and then use a nation id from the province id to lookup the nation record. This is a sensible thing to want and could be implemented, but is not currently supported.

4. Datasource names for joined tables are evaluated relative to the current processes working directory, not the path to the primary datasource.

5. These are not true LEFT or RIGHT joins in the RDBMS sense. Whether or not a secondary record exists for the join key or not, one and only one copy of the primary record is returned in the result set. If a secondary record cannot be found, the secondary derived fields will be NULL. If more than one matching secondary field is found only the first will be used.

UNION ALL

(OGR >= 1.10.0)

The SQL engine can deal with several `SELECT` combined with `UNION ALL`. The effect of `UNION ALL` is to concatenate the rows returned by the right `SELECT` statement to the rows returned by the left `SELECT` statement.

```
[(] SELECT field_list FROM first_layer [WHERE where_expr] [)]
UNION ALL [(] SELECT field_list FROM second_layer [WHERE where_expr] [)
[UNION ALL [(] SELECT field_list FROM third_layer [WHERE where_expr] [)
```

UNION ALL restrictions

The processing of UNION ALL in OGR differs from the SQL standard, in which it allows the columns from the various SELECT to not be identical. In that case, it will return a super-set of all the fields from each SELECT statement.

There is also a restriction : ORDER BY can only be specified for each SELECT, and not at the level of the result of the union.

SPECIAL FIELDS

The OGR SQL query processor treats some of the attributes of the features as built-in special fields which can be used in the SQL statements just like other normal fields.

These fields can be placed in the select list, the WHERE clause and the ORDER BY clause respectively. The special field will not be included in the result by default but it may be explicitly included by adding it to the select list. When accessing the field values the special fields will take precedence over the other fields with the same names in the data source.

FID

Normally the feature id is a special property of a feature and not treated as an attribute of the feature. In some cases it is convenient to be able to utilize the feature id in queries and result sets as a regular field. To do so, use the name FID. The field wildcard expansions will not include the feature id, but it may be explicitly included using a syntax like:

```
SELECT FID, * FROM nation
```

OGR_GEOMETRY

Some of the data sources (like MapInfo tab) can handle geometries of different types within the same layer. The `OGR_GEOMETRY` special field represents the geometry type returned by the `OGRGeometry::getGeometryName()` method and can be used to distinguish the various types. By using this field one can select particular types of the geometries like:

```
SELECT * FROM nation WHERE OGR_GEOMETRY='POINT' OR OGR_GEOMETRY='POLYGON'
```

OGR_GEOM_WKT

The Well Known Text representation of the geometry can also be used as a special field. To select the WKT of the geometry `OGR_GEOM_WKT` might be included in the select list, like:

```
SELECT OGR_GEOM_WKT, * FROM nation
```

Using the `OGR_GEOM_WKT` and the `LIKE` operator in the `WHERE` clause we can get similar effect as using `OGR_GEOMETRY`:

```
SELECT OGR_GEOM_WKT, * FROM nation WHERE OGR_GEOM_WKT
    LIKE 'POINT%' OR OGR_GEOM_WKT LIKE 'POLYGON%'
```

OGR_GEOM_AREA

(Since GDAL 1.7.0)

The `OGR_GEOM_AREA` special field returns the area of the feature's geometry computed by the `OGRSurface::get_Area()` method. For `OGRGeometryCollection` and `OGRMultiPolygon` the value is the sum of the areas of its members. For non-surface geometries the returned area is `0.0`.

For example, to select only polygon features larger than a given area:

```
SELECT * FROM nation WHERE 'OGR_GEOM_AREA > 10000000'
```

OGR_STYLE

The OGR_STYLE special field represents the style string of the feature returned by OGRFeature::GetStyleString(). By using this field and the LIKE operator the result of the query can be filtered by the style. For example, we can select the annotation features as:

```
SELECT * FROM nation WHERE OGR_STYLE LIKE 'LABEL%'
```

CREATE INDEX

Some OGR SQL drivers support creating of attribute indexes. Currently this includes the Shapefile driver. An index accelerates very simple attribute queries of the form fieldname = value, as used by the JOIN capability. For example, to create an attribute index on the nation_id field of the nation layer:

```
CREATE INDEX ON nation USING nation_id
```

Index Limitations

1. Indexes are not maintained dynamically when new features are added to or removed from a layer.

2. Very long strings (i.e. longer than 256 characters) cannot currently be indexed.

3. To recreate an index it is necessary to drop all indexes on a layer and then recreate all the indexes.

4. Indexes are not used in any complex queries. Currently the only query the will accelerate is a simple field = value query.

DROP INDEX

The OGR SQL DROP INDEX command can be used to drop all indexes on a particular table, or just the index for a particular column.

```
DROP INDEX ON nation USING nation_id
DROP INDEX ON nation
```

ALTER TABLE

(OGR >= 1.9.0)

The following OGR SQL ALTER TABLE commands can be used as follows:

1. ALTER TABLE tablename ADD [COLUMN] columnname columntype
   to add a new field. Supported if the layer declares the OLCCreateField capability.

2. ALTER TABLE tablename RENAME [COLUMN] oldcolumnname TO
   newcolumnname to rename an existing field. Supported if the layer declares the OLCAlterFieldDefn capability.

3. ALTER TABLE tablename ALTER [COLUMN] columnname TYPE columntype
   to change the type of an existing field. Supported if the layer declares the OLCAlterFieldDefn capability.

4. ALTER TABLE tablename DROP [COLUMN] columnname to delete
   an existing field. Supported if the layer declares the OLCDeleteField capability.

The columntype value follows the syntax of the types supported by the CAST operator described above.

```
ALTER TABLE nation ADD COLUMN myfield integer
ALTER TABLE nation RENAME COLUMN myfield TO myfield2
ALTER TABLE nation ALTER COLUMN myfield2 TYPE character(15)
ALTER TABLE nation DROP COLUMN myfield2
```

DROP TABLE

(OGR >= 1.9.0)

The OGR SQL DROP TABLE command can be used to delete a table. This is only supported on datasources that declare the ODsCDeleteLayer capability.

```
DROP TABLE nation
```

ExecuteSQL()

SQL is executed against an OGRDataSource, not against a specific layer. The call looks like this:

```
OGRLayer * OGRDataSource::ExecuteSQL( const char *pszSQLCommand,
                                      OGRGeometry *poSpatialFilter,
                                      const char *pszDialect );
```

The pszDialect argument is in theory intended to allow for support of different command languages against a provider, but for now applications should always pass an empty (not NULL) string to get the default dialect.

The poSpatialFilter argument is a geometry used to select a bounding rectangle for features to be returned in a manner similar to the OGRLayer::SetSpatialFilter() method. It may be NULL for no special spatial restriction.

The result of an ExecuteSQL() call is usually a temporary OGRLayer representing the results set from the statement. This is the case for a SELECT statement for instance. The returned temporary layer should be released with OGRDataSource::ReleaseResultsSet() method when no longer needed. Failure to release it before the datasource is destroyed may result in a crash.

Non-OGR SQL

All OGR drivers for database systems: MySQL, PostgreSQL and PostGIS (PG), Oracle (OCI), SQLite, ODBC, ESRI Personal Geodatabase (PGeo) and MS SQL Spatial (MSSQLSpatial), override the OGRDataSource::ExecuteSQL() function with a dedicated implementation and, by default, pass the SQL statements directly to the underlying RDBMS. In these cases the SQL syntax varies in some particulars from OGR SQL. Also, anything possible in SQL can then be accomplished for these particular databases. Only the result of SQL WHERE statements will be returned as layers.

Part VII

CSV File & VRT XML Formats

1

Comma Separated Value (.csv)

OGR supports reading and writing primarily non-spatial tabular data stored in text CSV files. CSV files are a common interchange format between software packages supporting tabular data and are also easily produced manually with a text editor or with end-user written scripts or programs.

While in theory CSV files could have any extension, in order to auto-recognise the format OGR only supports CSV files ending with the extension .csv.

The datasource name may be either a single CSV file or point to a directory. For a directory to be recognised as a CSV datasource at least half the files in the directory need to have the extension .csv. One layer (table) is produced from each CSV file accessed.

Starting with GDAL 1.8.0, for files structured as CSV, but not ending with .csv extension, the CSV: prefix can be added before the filename to force loading by the CSV driver. For example:

```
ogrinfo CSV:airports.txt
```

The OGR CSV driver supports reading and writing. Because the CSV format has variable length text lines, reading is done sequentially.

OGR CSV layers never have a coordinate system. When reading a field named WKT it is assumed to contain WKT geometry, but also is treated as a regular field. The OGR CSV driver returns all attribute columns as string data types unless a field type information file (.csvt) is available.

Limited type recognition can be done for Integer, Real, String, Date (YYYY-MM-DD), Time (HH:MM:SS+nn) and DateTime (YYYY-MM-DD HH:MM:SS+nn) columns using a descriptive file with the same name as the CSV file, but with a .csvt extension. In a single line the types for each column have to be listed using double quotes and separated by commas:

```
"Integer","String"
```

It is also possible to explicitly specify the width and precision of each column:

```
"Integer(5)","Real(10.7)","String(15)"
```

The driver will then use these types as specified for the CSV columns.

Format

CSV files have one line for each feature (record) in the layer (table). The attribute field values are separated by commas. At least two fields per line must be present. Lines may be terminated by a DOS (CR/LF) or Unix (LF) style line terminators. Each record should have the same number of fields.

Starting with GDAL 1.7.0, the driver will also accept a semicolon or a tabulation character as field separator. This auto-detection will work only if there is no other potential separator on the first line of the CSV file. Otherwise it will default to comma as separator.

Complex attribute values (such as those containing commas, quotes or newlines) may be placed in double quotes. Any occurrences of double quotes within the quoted string should be doubled up to "escape" them:

```
ID,Salary,Name,Comments
132,55000.0,John Walker,"The ""big"" cheese."
133,11000.0,Jane Lake,Cleaning Staff
```

Note that the Comments value for the first data record is placed in double quotes because the value contains quotes, and those quotes have to be doubled up so we know we haven't reached the end of the quoted string yet.

The driver attempts to treat the first line of the file as a list of field names for all the fields. However, if one or more of the names is all numeric it is assumed that the first line is actually data values and dummy field names are generated internally (field_1 through field_n) and the first record is treated as a feature. Starting with GDAL 1.9.0 numeric values are treated as field names if they are enclosed in double quotes.

All CSV files are treated as UTF–8 encoded. Starting with GDAL 1.9.0, a Byte Order Mark (BOM) at the beginning of the file will be parsed correctly. From 1.9.2, The option WRITE_BOM can be used to create a file with a Byte Order Mark, which can improve compatibility with some software (particularly Excel).

Many variations of textual input are sometimes called *Comma Separated Value* files, including files **without commas**, but fixed column widths, those using tabs as separators, or those with other auxiliary data defining field types or structure. This driver does not attempt to support all such files, but instead to support simple .csv files that can be auto-recognised. Scripts or other mechanisms can generally be used to convert other variations into a form that is compatible with the OGR CSV driver.

Reading point data From a CSV file using the VRT driver

It is possible to extract spatial information (points) from a CSV file which has columns for the X and Y coordinates, through the use of the VRT driver.[90]

[90] See the *OGR VRT - Virtual Format* chapter on page 295.

Consider the following CSV file (test.csv):

```
Latitude,Longitude,Name
48.1,0.25,"First point"
49.2,1.1,"Second point"
47.5,0.75,"Third point"
```

You can write the associated VRT file (test.vrt):

```
<OGRVRTDataSource>
    <OGRVRTLayer name="test">
        <SrcDataSource>test.csv</SrcDataSource>
        <GeometryType>wkbPoint</GeometryType>
        <LayerSRS>WGS84</LayerSRS>
        <GeometryField encoding="PointFromColumns"
                        x="Longitude" y="Latitude"/>
    </OGRVRTLayer>
</OGRVRTDataSource>
```

and *ogrinfo -ro -al test.vrt* will return:

```
OGRFeature(test):1
  Latitude (String) = 48.1
  Longitude (String) = 0.25
  Name (String) = First point
  POINT (0.25 48.1 0)

OGRFeature(test):2
  Latitude (String) = 49.2
  Longitude (String) = 1.1
  Name (String) = Second point
  POINT (1.1 49.200000000000003 0)

OGRFeature(test):3
  Latitude (String) = 47.5
  Longitude (String) = 0.75
  Name (String) = Third point
  POINT (0.75 47.5 0)
```

Creation Issues

The driver supports creating new databases (as a directory of CSV files), adding new CSV files to an existing directory of CSV files or appending features to an existing CSV table. Deleting or replacing existing features is not supported.

Layer creation options can be specified using the OGR -lco NAME=VALUE command line syntax. The following options apply to CSV files:

LINEFORMAT
By default when creating new .csv files they are created with the line termination conventions of the local platform (CR/LF on win32 or LF on all other systems). This may be overridden through use of the LINEFORMAT layer creation option which may have a value of **CRLF** (DOS format) or **LF** (Unix format).

GEOMETRY [v1.6+]
By default, the geometry of a feature written to a .csv file is discarded. It is possible to export the geometry in its WKT representation by specifying GEOMETRY=AS_WKT. It is also possible to export point geometries into their X,Y,Z components (different columns in the CSV file) by specifying GEOMETRY=AS_XYZ, GEOMETRY=AS_XY or GEOMETRY=AS_YX. The geometry column(s) will be prepended to the columns with the attributes values.

CREATE_CSVT=YES/NO [v1.7+]
Create the associated .csvt file (see earlier paragraph) to describe the type of each column of the layer and its optional width and precision.

Default value: NO.

SEPARATOR=COMMA/SEMICOLON/TAB [v1.7+]
Field separator character. Default value: COMMA.

WRITE_BOM=YES/NO [v1.9.2+]
Write a UTF–8 Byte Order Mark (BOM) at the start of the file. Default value: NO.

Examples

This example shows using `ogr2ogr` to transform a shapefile with point geometry into a CSV file with the X,Y,Z coordinates of the points as first columns in the file:

```
ogr2ogr -f CSV output.csv input.shp -lco GEOMETRY=AS_XYZ
```

Particular datasources

The CSV driver can also read files whose structure is close to CSV files:

- US FAA Airport data files - NFDC facility, runway, remark and schedule XLS files found on the FAA safety website. [v1.8+][91]

- Files from the USGS GNIS (Geographic Names Information System) [v1.9+][92]

- The *allCountries* file from GeoNames [v1.9+] for direct import.[93]

- Eurostat .TSV files [v1.10+][94]

Other Notes

Development of the OGR CSV driver was supported by DM Solutions Group[95] and GoMOOS.[96]

[91] FAA Airport Data: http://loc8.cc/gpt/faa_data

[92] USGS GNIS: http://loc8.cc/gpt/gnis

[93] GeoNames: http://geonames.org

[94] Eurostat files: http://loc8.cc/gpt/eurostat

[95] http://dmsolutions.ca
[96] http://gomoos.org

2

OGR VRT - Virtual Format

OGR Virtual Format is a driver that transforms features read from other drivers based on criteria specified in an XML control file. It is primarily used to derive spatial layers from flat tables with spatial information in attribute columns. It can also be used to associate co-ordinate system information with a datasource, merge layers from different datasources into a single data source, or even to just provide an anchor file for access to non-file oriented datasources.

An OGR VRT file is normally prepared by hand using a text editor.

Creation Issues

Prior to GDAL 1.7.0, the OGR VRT driver was read-only.

Since GDAL 1.7.0, the create, set and delete feature operations are supported on a layer of a VRT dataset, if the following conditions are met:

- the VRT dataset is opened in update mode
- the underlying source layer supports those operations
- the SrcLayer element is used (as opposed to the SrcSQL element)
- the FID of the VRT features is the same as the FID of the source features, that is to say, the FID element is not specified

Virtual File XML Structure

The root element of the XML control file is **OGRVRTDataSource**. It has an **OGRVRTLayer**[97] child element for each layer in the virtual datasource.

[97] **[v1.10+]** Root element may also be **OGRVRTWarpedLayer** or **OGRVRTUnion-Layer**

An **OGRVRTLayer** element should have a **name** attribute with the layer name, and may have the following subelements:

SrcDataSource (mandatory):

The value is the name of the datasource that this layer will be derived from. The element may optionally have a **relativeToVRT** attribute which defaults to 0, but if 1 indicates that the source datasource should be interpreted as relative to the virtual file. This can be any OGR supported dataset, including ODBC, CSV, etc. The element may also have a **shared** attribute to control whether the datasource should be opened in shared mode. Defaults to OFF for SrcLayer use and ON for SrcSQL use.

SrcLayer (optional):

The value is the name of the layer on the source data source from which this virtual layer should be derived. If this element isn't provided, then the SrcSQL element must be provided.

SrcSQL (optional):

An SQL statement to execute to generate the desired layer result. This should be provided instead of the SrcLayer for statement derived results. Some limitations may apply for SQL derived layers. Starting with OGR 1.10, an optional **dialect** attribute can be specified on the SrcSQL element to specify which SQL "dialect" should be used : possible values are currently OGRSQL[98] or SQLITE.[99] If *dialect* is not specified, the default dialect of the datasource will be used.

[98] OGR SQL: http://loc8.cc/ogr_sql
[99] SQLite: http://loc8.cc/gpt/sqlite

FID (optional):

Name of the attribute column from which the FID of features

should be derived. If not provided, the FID of the source features will be used directly.

Style *(optional):*

Name of the attribute column from which the style of features should be derived. If not provided, the style of the source features will be used directly.

GeometryType *(optional):*

The geometry type to be assigned to the layer. If not provided it will be taken from the source layer. The value should be one of wkbNone, wkbUnknown, wkbPoint, wkbLineString, wkbPolygon, wkbMultiPoint, wkbMultiLineString, wkbMultiPolygon, or wkbGeometryCollection. Optionally 25D may be appended to mark it as including Z coordinates. By default, wkbUnknown is used indicating that any geometry type is allowed.

LayerSRS *(optional):*

The value of this element is the spatial reference to use for the layer. If not provided, it is inherited from the source layer.[100] If the value is NULL, then no SRS will be used for the layer.

GeometryField *(optional):*

This element is used to define how the geometry for features should be derived. If not provided the geometry of the source feature is copied directly.

The type of geometry encoding is indicated with the **encoding** attribute which may have the value WKT, WKB or PointFromColumns.

If the encoding is WKT or WKB then the **field** attribute will have the name of the field containing the WKT or WKB geometry. If the encoding is PointFromColumns then the **x**, **y** and **z** attributes will have the names of the columns to be used for the X, Y and Z coordinates. The **z** attribute is optional.

Starting with GDAL 1.7.0, the optional **reportSrcColumn** attribute

---

[100] The value may be WKT or any other input that is accepted by the OGRSpatialReference::SetUserInput() method.

can be used to specify whether the source geometry fields (the fields set in the **field, x, x** or **z** attributes) should be reported as fields of the VRT layer. It defaults to TRUE. If set to FALSE, the source geometry fields will only be used to build the geometry of the features of the VRT layer.

SrcRegion (optional, [v1.7+]):

This element is used to define an initial spatial filter for the source features. This spatial filter will be combined with any spatial filter explicitly set on the VRT layer with the SetSpatialFilter() method. The value of the element must be a valid WKT string defining a polygon. An optional **clip** attribute can be set to "TRUE" to clip the geometries to the source region, otherwise the source geometries are not modified.

Field (optional, [v1.7+]):

One or more attribute fields may be defined with Field elements. If no field elements are defined, the fields of the source layer/sql will be defined on the VRT layer. The field may have the following attributes:

- **name** (required): the name of the field.
- **type**: the field type, one of Integer, IntegerList, Real, RealList, String, StringList, Binary, Date, Time, or DateTime - defaults to String.
- **width**: the field width, defaults to unknown.
- **precision**: the field width, defaults to zero.
- **src**: the name of the source field to be copied to this one. By default defaults to the value of name.

FeatureCount (optional, [v1.10+]):

This element is used to define the feature count of the layer (when no spatial or attribute filter is set). This can be useful on static data, when getting the feature count from the source layer is slow.

ExtentXMin, ExtentYMin, ExtentXMax and ExtentXMax
(optional, **[v1.10+]**): Those elements are used to define the extent of the layer. This can be useful on static data, when getting the extent from the source layer is slow.

A **OGRVRTWarpedLayer** element (**[v1.10+]**) is used to do on-the-fly reprojection of a source layer. It may have the following subelements:

OGRVRTLayer, OGRVRTWarpedLayer or OGRVRTUnionLayer
(mandatory): the source layer to reproject.

SrcSRS (mandatory):
The value of this element is the spatial reference to use for the layer before reprojection. If not specified, it is deduced from the source layer.

TargetSRS (mandatory):
The value of this element is the spatial reference to use for the layer after reprojection.

ExtentXMin, ExtentYMin, ExtentXMax and ExtentXMax
(optional, **[v1.10+]**): Those elements are used to define the extent of the layer. This can be useful on static data, when getting the extent from the source layer is slow.

A **OGRVRTUnionLayer** element (**[v1.10+]**) is used to concatenate the content of source layers. It should have a **name** and may have the following subelements:

OGRVRTLayer, OGRVRTWarpedLayer or OGRVRTUnionLayer
(mandatory and may be repeated): a source layer to add in the union.

PreserveSrcFID (optional):
may be ON or OFF. If set to ON, the *FID* from the source layer will be used, otherwise a counter will be used. Defaults to OFF.

SourceLayerFieldName (optional):

if specified, an additional field (named with the value of *Source-LayerFieldName*) will be added in the layer field definition. For each feature, the value of this field will be set with the name of the layer from which the feature comes from.

GeometryType (optional):

see above for the syntax. If not specified, the geometry type will be deduced from the geometry type of all source layers.

LayerSRS (optional):

see above for the syntax. If not specified, the SRS will be the SRS of the first source layer.

*FieldStrategy (optional, exclusive with **Field**) :*

may be **FirstLayer** to use the fields from the first layer found, **Union** to use a super-set of all the fields from all source layers, or **Intersection** to use a sub-set of all the common fields from all source layers. Defaults to **Union**.

*Field (optional, exclusive with **FieldStrategy**):*

see above for the syntax. Note: the *src* attribute is not supported in the context of a *OGRVRTUnionLayer* element (field names are assumed to be identical).

FeatureCount (optional):

see above for the syntax

ExtentXMin, ExtentYMin, ExtentXMax and ExtentXMax

(optional): see above for the syntax

Example: ODBC Point Layer

In the following example (`disease.ovf`) the worms table from the ODBC database `DISEASE` is used to form a spatial layer. The virtual file uses the "x" and "y" columns to get the spatial location. It also marks the layer as a point layer, and as being in the WGS84 coordinate system.

```
<OGRVRTDataSource>
  <OGRVRTLayer name="worms">
    <SrcDataSource>ODBC:DISEASE,worms</SrcDataSource>
    <SrcLayer>worms</SrcLayer>
    <GeometryType>wkbPoint</GeometryType>
    <LayerSRS>WGS84</LayerSRS>
    <GeometryField encoding="PointFromColumns" x="x" y="y"/>
  </OGRVRTLayer>
</OGRVRTDataSource>
```

Example: Renaming attributes

It can be useful in some circumstances to be able to rename the field
names from a source layer to other names. This is particularly true
when you want to transcode to a format whose schema is fixed,
such as GPX (<name>, <desc>, etc.). This can be accomplished using
SQL this way:

```
<OGRVRTDataSource>
  <OGRVRTLayer name="remapped_layer">
    <SrcDataSource>your_source.shp</SrcDataSource>
    <SrcSQL>SELECT src_field_1 AS name, src_field_2 AS desc
            FROM your_source_layer_name</SrcSQL>
  </OGRVRTLayer>
</OGRVRTDataSource>
```

This can also be accomplished ([v1.7+]) using explicit field definitions:

```
<OGRVRTDataSource>
  <OGRVRTLayer name="remapped_layer">
    <SrcDataSource>your_source.shp</SrcDataSource>
    <SrcLayer>your_source</SrcSQL>
      <Field name="name" src="src_field_1" />
      <Field name="desc" src="src_field_2" type="String"
      width="45" />
  </OGRVRTLayer>
</OGRVRTDataSource>
```

Example: Transparent spatial filtering ([v1.7+])

The following example will only return features from the source layer that intersect the (0,40)-(10,50) region. Furthermore, returned geometries will be clipped to fit into that region.

```
<OGRVRTDataSource>
  <OGRVRTLayer name="source">
    <SrcDataSource>source.shp</SrcDataSource>
    <SrcRegion clip="true">
      POLYGON((0 40,10 40,10 50,0 50,0 40))
    </SrcRegion>
  </OGRVRTLayer>
</OGRVRTDataSource>
```

Example: Reprojected layer ([v1.10+])

The following example will return the source.shp layer reprojected to EPSG:4326.

```
<OGRVRTDataSource>
  <OGRVRTWarpedLayer>
    <OGRVRTLayer name="source">
      <SrcDataSource>source.shp</SrcDataSource>
    </OGRVRTLayer>
      <TargetSRS>EPSG:4326</TargetSRS>
  </OGRVRTWarpedLayer>
</OGRVRTDataSource>
```

Example: Union layer ([v1.10+])

The following example will return a layer that is the concatenation of source1.shp and source2.shp.

```
<OGRVRTDataSource>
  <OGRVRTUnionLayer name="unionLayer">
    <OGRVRTLayer name="source1">
      <SrcDataSource>source1.shp</SrcDataSource>
    </OGRVRTLayer>
    <OGRVRTLayer name="source2">
      <SrcDataSource>source2.shp</SrcDataSource>
```

```
    </OGRVRTLayer>
   </OGRVRTUnionLayer>
  </OGRVRTDataSource>
```

Example: SQLite/SpatiaLite SQL dialect ([v1.10+])

The following example will return four different layers which are generated on the fly from the same polygon shapefile. The first one is the shapefile layer as it stands. The second layer, gives simplified polygons by applying SpatiaLite function "Simplify" with parameter tolerance=10. In the third layer, the original geometries are replaced by their convex hulls. In the fourth layer, the SpatiaLite function *PointOnSurface* is used for replacing the original geometries by points which are inside the corresponding source polygons. Note that for using the last three layers of this VRT file, GDAL must be compiled with SQLite and SpatiaLite support.

```
<OGRVRTDataSource>
  <OGRVRTLayer name="polygons">
    <SrcDataSource>polygons.shp</SrcDataSource>
  </OGRVRTLayer>
  <OGRVRTLayer name="polygons_as_simplified">
    <SrcDataSource>polygons.shp</SrcDataSource>
    <SrcSQL dialect="sqlite">
      SELECT Simplify(geometry,10) from polygons
        </SrcSQL>
  </OGRVRTLayer>
  <OGRVRTLayer name="polygons_as_hulls">
    <SrcDataSource>polygons.shp</SrcDataSource>
    <SrcSQL dialect="sqlite">
            SELECT ConvexHull(geometry) from polygons
    </SrcSQL>
  </OGRVRTLayer>
  <OGRVRTLayer name="polygons_as_points">
    <SrcDataSource>polygons.shp</SrcDataSource>
    <SrcSQL dialect="sqlite">
      SELECT PointOnSurface(geometry) from polygons
        </SrcSQL>
```

```
        </OGRVRTLayer>
    </OGRVRTDataSource>
```

Other Notes

When the GeometryField *is* WKT, *spatial filtering is applied after* extracting all rows from the source datasource. Essentially, this means there is no fast spatial filtering on WKT derived geometries.

When the GeometryField *is* PointFromColumns, *and a* SrcLayer *(as* opposed to *SrcSQL*) is used, and a spatial filter is in effect on the virtual layer then the spatial filter will be internally translated into an attribute filter on the X and Y columns in the *SrcLayer*. In cases where fast spatial filtering is important it can be helpful to index the X and Y columns in the source datastore, if that is possible (for example, the source is an RDBMS). You can turn off that feature by setting the *useSpatialSubquery* attribute of the *GeometryField* element to FALSE.

3

GDAL VRT - Virtual Format

Introduction

The VRT driver is a format driver for GDAL that allows a virtual dataset to be composed from other GDAL datasets with repositioning, and algorithms potentially applied, as well as various kinds of metadata altered or added. VRT descriptions of datasets can be saved in an XML format normally given the extension .vrt.

An example of a simple .vrt file referring to a 512x512 dataset with one band loaded from utm.tif might look like this:

```
<VRTDataset rasterXSize="512" rasterYSize="512">
  <GeoTransform>
    440720.0, 60.0, 0.0, 3751320.0, 0.0, -60.0
  </GeoTransform>
  <VRTRasterBand dataType="Byte" band="1">
    <ColorInterp>Gray</ColorInterp>
    <SimpleSource>
      <SourceFilename relativeToVRT="1">
        utm.tif
      </SourceFilename>
      <SourceBand>1</SourceBand>
      <SrcRect xOff="0" yOff="0" xSize="512" ySize="512"/>
      <DstRect xOff="0" yOff="0" xSize="512" ySize="512"/>
```

```
    </SimpleSource>
  </VRTRasterBand>
</VRTDataset>
```

Many aspects of the VRT file are a direct XML encoding of the *GDAL Data Model*[101] which should be reviewed for understanding of the semantics of various elements.

[101] GDAL Data Model: `http://loc8.cc/gpt/gdaldm`

VRT files can be produced by translating to VRT format. The resulting file can then be edited to modify mappings, add metadata or other purposes. VRT files can also be produced programmatically by various means.

This tutorial will cover the VRT file format (suitable for users editing VRT files), and how .vrt files may be created and manipulated programmatically for developers.

.vrt Format

Virtual files stored on disk are kept in an XML format with the following elements.

VRTDataset: This is the root element for the whole GDAL dataset. It must have the attributes *rasterXSize* and *rasterYSize* describing the width and height of the dataset in pixels. It may have *SRS*, *GeoTransform*, *GCPList*, *Metadata*, *MaskBand* and *VRTRasterBand* subelements.

```
<VRTDataset rasterXSize="512" rasterYSize="512">
```

The allowed subelements for `VRTDataset` are:

SRS:

This element contains the spatial reference system (coordinate system) in OGC WKT format. Note that this must be appropriately escaped for XML, so items like quotes will have the ampersand escape sequences substituted. As well as WKT, valid input to the `SetFromUserInput()` method (such as well known GEOGCS names, and PROJ.4 format) is allowed in the SRS element:

```
<SRS>PROJCS[NAD27 / UTM zone 11
  GEOGCS[NAD27,DATUM[North_American_Datum_1927,
    SPHEROID[Clarke 1866,6378206.4,294.9786982139006,
    AUTHORITY[EPSG,7008]],
    AUTHORITY[EPSG,6267]],
    PRIMEM[Greenwich,0],
    UNIT[degree,0.0174532925199433],
    AUTHORITY[EPSG,4267]],
  PROJECTION[Transverse_Mercator],
  PARAMETER[latitude_of_origin,0],
  PARAMETER[central_meridian,-117],
  PARAMETER[scale_factor,0.9996],
  ...
</SRS>
```

GeoTransform:

This element contains a six value affine geotransformation for the dataset, mapping between pixel/line coordinates and georeferenced coordinates:

```
<GeoTransform>
  440720.0, 60, 0.0, 3751320.0, 0.0, -60.0
</GeoTransform>
```

GCPList:

This element contains a list of Ground Control Points for the dataset, mapping between pixel/line coordinates and georeferenced coordinates. The Projection attribute should contain the SRS of the georeferenced coordinates in the same format as the SRS element:

```
<GCPList Projection="EPSG:4326">
  <GCP Id="1" Info="a" Pixel="0.5" Line="0.5"
       X="0.0" Y="0.0" Z="0.0" />
  <GCP Id="2" Info="b" Pixel="13.5" Line="23.5"
       X="1.0" Y="2.0" Z="0.0" />
</GCPList>
```

Metadata:

This element contains a list of metadata name/value pairs associated with the *VRTDataset* as a whole, or a *VRTRasterBand*. It has the *MDI* (metadata item) subelements which have a key attribute and the value as the data of the element:

```
<Metadata>
  <MDI key="md_key">Metadata value</MDI>
</Metadata>
```

MaskBand ([v1.8+]):

This element represents a mask band that is shared between all bands on the dataset. It must contain a single *VRTRasterBand* child element that describes the mask band:

```
<MaskBand>
  <VRTRasterBand dataType="Byte">
    <SimpleSource>
      <SourceFilename relativeToVRT="1">
        utm.tif
      </SourceFilename>
      <SourceBand>mask,1</SourceBand>
      <SrcRect xOff="0" yOff="0" xSize="512" ySize="512"/>
      <DstRect xOff="0" yOff="0" xSize="512" ySize="512"/>
    </SimpleSource>
  </VRTRasterBand>
</MaskBand>
```

[102] Use names Byte, UInt16, Int16, UInt32, Int32, Float32, Float64, CInt16, CInt32, CFloat32 or CFloat64.

VRTRasterBand:

This represents one band of a dataset. It will have a *dataType* attribute with the type of the pixel data associated with the band[102] and the band this element represents (1 based). This element may have *Metadata, ColorInterp, NoDataValue, HideNoDataValue, ColorTable, Description* and *MaskBand* subelements as well as the various kinds of source elements such as *SimpleSource, ComplexSource,* etc. A raster band may have many sources indicating where the actual raster data should be fetched from, and how it should be mapped into the raster bands pixel space.

The allowed subelements for VRTRasterBand are:

ColorInterp:

The data of this element should be the name of a color interpretation type; one of Gray, Palette, Red, Green, Blue, Alpha, Hue, Saturation, Lightness, Cyan, Magenta, Yellow, Black, or Unknown.

```
<ColorInterp>Gray</ColorInterp>
```

NoDataValue:

If this element exists, the raster band has a nodata value associated with it, the value given as data in the element:

```
<NoDataValue>-100.0</NoDataValue>
```

HideNoDataValue:

If this value is 1, the nodata value will not be reported. Essentially, the caller will not be aware of a nodata pixel when it reads one. Any datasets copied/translated from this will not have a nodata value. This is useful when you want to specify a fixed background value for the dataset. The background will be the value specified by the *NoDataValue* element.

Default value is 0 when this element is absent.

```
<HideNoDataValue>1</HideNoDataValue>
```

ColorTable:

This element is parent to a set of *Entry* elements defining the entries in a color table. Currently only RGBA color tables are supported with c1 being red, c2 being green, c3 being blue and c4 being alpha. The entries are ordered and will be assumed to start from color table entry 0.

```
<ColorTable>
  <Entry c1="0" c2="0" c3="0" c4="255"/>
  <Entry c1="145" c2="78" c3="224" c4="255"/>
</ColorTable>
```

Description:

This element contains an optional description of a raster band as a text value.

```
<Description>Crop Classification Layer</Description>
```

UnitType:

This optional element contains the vertical units for elevation band data; one of m for meters or ft for feet. Default assumption is meters.

```
<UnitType>ft</UnitType>
```

Offset:

This optional element contains the offset that should be applied when computing "real" pixel values from scaled pixel values on a raster band. The default is 0.0.

```
<Offset>0.0</Offset>
```

Scale:

This optional element contains the scale that should be applied when computing "real" pixel values from scaled pixel values on a raster band. The default is 1.0.

```
<Scale>1.0</Scale>
```

Overview:

This optional element describes one overview level for the band. It should have a child *SourceFilename* and *SourceBand* element. The *SourceFilename* may have a *relativeToVRT* boolean attribute. Multiple elements may be used to describe multiple overviews.

```
<Overview>
  <SourceFilename relativeToVRT="1">
    yellowstone_2.1.ntf.r2
  </SourceFilename>
  <SourceBand>1</SourceBand>
</Overview>
```

CategoryNames:

This optional element contains a list of *Category* subelements with the names of the categories for the classified raster band.

```
<CategoryNames>
  <Category>Missing</Category>
  <Category>Non-Crop</Category>
  <Category>Wheat</Category>
  <Category>Corn</Category>
  <Category>Soybeans</Category>
</CategoryNames>
```

SimpleSource:

The *SimpleSource* indicates that raster data should be read from a separate dataset, indicating the dataset, and band to be read from, and how the data should map into this bands raster space. The *SimpleSource* may have the *SourceFilename, Source-Band, SrcRect*, and *DstRect* subelements. The *SrcRect* element will indicate what rectangle on the indicated source file should be read, and the *DstRect* element indicates how that rectangle of source data should be mapped into the *VRTRasterBands* space.

The *relativeToVRT* attribute on the *SourceFilename* indicates whether the filename should be interpreted as relative to the .vrt file (value is 1) or not relative to the .vrt file (value is 0). The default is 0.

Some characteristics of the source band can be specified in the optional *SourceProperties* tag to enable the VRT driver to defer opening of the source dataset until it really needs to read data from it. This is particularly useful when building VRTs with a big number of source datasets. The needed parameters are the raster dimensions, the size of the blocks and the data type. If the *SourceProperties* tag is not present, the source dataset will be opened at the same time as the VRT itself.

Starting with GDAL 1.8.0, the content of the *SourceBand* subelement can refer to a mask band. For example mask, 1 means the mask band of the first band of the source.

```
<SimpleSource>
  <SourceFilename relativeToVRT="1">
                  utm.tif</SourceFilename>
  <SourceBand>1</SourceBand>
  <SourceProperties RasterXSize="512" RasterYSize="512"
                    DataType="Byte"
                    BlockXSize="128" BlockYSize="128"/>
  <SrcRect xOff="0" yOff="0" xSize="512" ySize="512"/>
  <DstRect xOff="0" yOff="0" xSize="512" ySize="512"/>
</SimpleSource>
```

AveragedSource:

The *AveragedSource* is derived from the *SimpleSource* and shares the same properties except that it uses an averaging resampling instead of a nearest neighbour algorithm as in *Simple-Source*, when the size of the destination rectangle is not the same as the size of the source rectangle

ComplexSource:

The *ComplexSource* is derived from the *SimpleSource* (so it shares the *SourceFilename*, *SourceBand*, *SrcRect* and *DestRect* elements), but it provides support to rescale and offset the range of the source values. Certain regions of the source can be masked by specifying the NODATA value.

Starting with GDAL 2.0, alternatively to linear scaling, non-linear scaling using a power function can be used by specifying the *Exponent*, *SrcMin*, *SrcMax*, *DstMin* and *DstMax* elements. If *SrcMin* and *SrcMax* are not specified, they are computed from the source minimum and maximum value (which might require analyzing the whole source dataset). The exponent must be positive.[103]

[103] Those 5 values can be set with the -exponent and -scale options of gdal_translate.

The *ComplexSource* supports adding a custom lookup table

(LUT) to transform the source values to the destination. The LUT can be specified using the following form:

```
<LUT>[src value 1]:[dest value 1],
    [src value 2]:[dest value 2],
    ...
</LUT>
```

The intermediary values are calculated using a linear interpolation between the bounding destination values of the corresponding range.

The *ComplexSource* supports fetching a color component from a source raster band that has a color table. The *ColorTableComponent* value is the index of the color component to extract: 1 for the red band, 2 for the green band, 3 for the blue band or 4 for the alpha band.

When transforming the source values the operations are executed in the following order:

1. Nodata masking

2. Color table expansion

3. For linear scaling, applying the scale ratio, then scale offset

4. For non-linear scaling, apply:

```
(DstMax-DstMin) *
pow( (SrcValue-SrcMin) / (SrcMax-SrcMin), Exponent) +
DstMin
```

1. Table lookup

```
<ComplexSource>
  <SourceFilename relativeToVRT="1">
    utm.tif
  </SourceFilename>
  <SourceBand>1</SourceBand>
  <ScaleOffset>0</ScaleOffset>
```

```
<ScaleRatio>1</ScaleRatio>
<ColorTableComponent>1</ColorTableComponent>
<LUT>0:0,2345.12:64,56789.5:128,2364753.02:255</LUT>
<NODATA>0</NODATA>
<SrcRect xOff="0" yOff="0" xSize="512" ySize="512"/>
<DstRect xOff="0" yOff="0" xSize="512" ySize="512"/>
</ComplexSource>
```

1. Non-linear scaling:

```
<ComplexSource>
  <SourceFilename relativeToVRT="1">
    16bit.tif
  </SourceFilename>
  <SourceBand>1</SourceBand>
  <Exponent>0.75</Exponent>
  <SrcMin>0</SrcMin>
  <SrcMax>65535</SrcMax>
  <DstMin>0</DstMin>
  <DstMax>255</DstMax>
  <SrcRect xOff="0" yOff="0" xSize="512" ySize="512"/>
  <DstRect xOff="0" yOff="0" xSize="512" ySize="512"/>
</ComplexSource>
```

KernelFilteredSource:

This is a pixel source derived from the Simple Source (so it shares the *SourceFilename*, *SourceBand*, *SrcRect* and *DestRect* elements, but it also passes the data through a simple filtering kernel specified with the *Kernel* element. The *Kernel* element should have two child elements, *Size* and *Coefs* and optionally the boolean attribute normalized (defaults to `false=0`). The size must always be an odd number, and the *Coefs* must have `Size * Size` entries separated by spaces.

```
<KernelFilteredSource>
  <SourceFilename>utm.tif</SourceFilename>
  <SourceBand>1</SourceBand>
  <Kernel normalized="1">
    <Size>3</Size>
```

```
    <Coefs>0.11111111 0.11111111 0.11111111
            0.11111111 0.11111111 0.11111111
            0.11111111 0.11111111 0.11111111
    </Coefs>
    </Kernel>
  </KernelFilteredSource>
```

MaskBand ([v1.8+]):

This element represents a mask band that is specific to the *VRTRasterBand* it contains. It must contain a single *VRTRaster-Band* child element, that is the description of the mask band itself.

.vrt Descriptions for Raw Files

So far we have described how to derive new virtual datasets from existing files supported by GDAL. However, it is also common to need to utilize raw binary raster files for which the regular layout of the data is known but for which no format specific driver exists. This can be accomplished by writing a .vrt file describing the raw file.

For example, the following .vrt describes a raw raster file containing floating point complex pixels in a file called l2p3hhsso.img. The image data starts from the first byte (ImageOffset=0). The byte offset between pixels is 8 (PixelOffset=8), the size of a CFloat32. The byte offset from the start of one line to the start of the next is 9376 bytes (LineOffset=9376) which is the width (1172) times the size of a pixel (8).

```
<VRTDataset rasterXSize="1172" rasterYSize="1864">
  <VRTRasterBand dataType="CFloat32"
                band="1"
                subClass="VRTRawRasterBand">
    <SourceFilename relativetoVRT="1">
            l2p3hhsso.img
    </SourceFilename>
    <ImageOffset>0</ImageOffset>
```

```
        <PixelOffset>8</PixelOffset>
        <LineOffset>9376</LineOffset>
        <ByteOrder>MSB</ByteOrder>
      </VRTRasterBand>
    </VRTDataset>
```

Some things to note are that the *VRTRasterBand* has a *subClass* specifier of *VRTRawRasterBand*. Also, the *VRTRawRasterBand* contains a number of previously unseen elements but no source information. *VRTRawRasterBands* may never have sources (i.e. *SimpleSource*), but should contain the following elements in addition to all the normal metadata elements previously described which are still supported:

- **SourceFilename**: The name of the raw file containing the data for this band. The *relativeToVRT* attribute can be used to indicate if the *SourceFilename* is relative to the .vrt file (1) or not (0).
- **ImageOffset**: The offset in bytes to the beginning of the first pixel of data of this image band. Defaults to zero.
- **PixelOffset**: The offset in bytes from the beginning of one pixel and the next on the same line. In packed single band data this will be the size of the **dataType** in bytes.
- **LineOffset**: The offset in bytes from the beginning of one scanline of data and the next scanline of data. In packed single band data this will be PixelOffset * rasterXSize.
- **ByteOrder**: Defines the byte order of the data on disk. Either LSB (Least Significant Byte first) such as the natural byte order on Intel x86 systems or MSB (Most Significant Byte first) such as the natural byte order on Motorola or Sparc systems. Defaults to being the local machine order.

A few other notes:

- The image data on disk is assumed to be of the same data type as the band **dataType** of the *VRTRawRasterBand*.
- All the non-source attributes of the *VRTRasterBand* are supported, including color tables, metadata, nodata values, and color interpretation.
- The *VRTRawRasterBand* supports in-place update of the raster, whereas the source based *VRTRasterBand* is always read-only.

- The OpenEV tool[104] includes a File menu option to input parameters describing a raw raster file in a GUI and create the corresponding .vrt file.
- Multiple bands in a single .vrt file can come from the same raw file. Just ensure that the *ImageOffset*, *PixelOffset*, and *LineOffset* definition for each band is appropriate for the pixels of that particular band.

[104] OpenEV http://openev.sourceforge.net/

Here is another example; a 400x300 RGB pixel interleaved image:

```
<VRTDataset rasterXSize="400" rasterYSize="300">
  <VRTRasterBand dataType="Byte"
                band="1" subClass="VRTRawRasterBand">
    <ColorInterp>Red</ColorInterp>
    <SourceFilename relativetoVRT="1">rgb.raw</SourceFilename>
    <ImageOffset>0</ImageOffset>
    <PixelOffset>3</PixelOffset>
    <LineOffset>1200</LineOffset>
  </VRTRasterBand>
  <VRTRasterBand dataType="Byte"
                band="2" subClass="VRTRawRasterBand">
    <ColorInterp>Green</ColorInterp>
    <SourceFilename relativetoVRT="1">rgb.raw</SourceFilename>
    <ImageOffset>1</ImageOffset>
    <PixelOffset>3</PixelOffset>
    <LineOffset>1200</LineOffset>
  </VRTRasterBand>
  <VRTRasterBand dataType="Byte"
                band="3" subClass="VRTRawRasterBand">
    <ColorInterp>Blue</ColorInterp>
    <SourceFilename relativetoVRT="1">rgb.raw</SourceFilename>
    <ImageOffset>2</ImageOffset>
    <PixelOffset>3</PixelOffset>
    <LineOffset>1200</LineOffset>
  </VRTRasterBand>
</VRTDataset>
```

Programmatic Creation of VRT Datasets

The VRT driver supports several methods of creating VRT datasets. As of GDAL 1.2.0 the vrtdataset.h include file should be installed with the core GDAL include files, allowing direct access to the VRT classes. However, even without it, most capabilities remain available through standard GDAL interfaces.

For detailed C++ usage and in-depth examples, see the online documentation at http://loc8.cc/gpt/vrtcode.

Part VIII

Appendix 1 - Projection
Library Options

1

PROJ.4 - General Parameters

This chapter describes a variety of the PROJ.4 parameters which can be applied to all, or many coordinate system definitions—it does not attempt to describe parameters particular to certain projection types. Some of these can be found in the GeoTIFF Projections Transform List.[105] The definitive documentation for most parameters is the original documentation available from the main PROJ.4 page.[106]

[105] GeoTIFF Projections List: http://loc8.cc/projlist

[106] PROJ.4 site: http://loc8.cc/proj

False Easting/Northing

Virtually all coordinate systems allow for the presence of a false easting (+x_0) and northing (+y_0). Note that these values are always expressed in meters even if the coordinate system is in some other units. Some coordinate systems (such as UTM) have implicit false easting and northing values.

pm - Prime Meridian

A prime meridian may be declared indicating the offset between the prime meridian of the declared coordinate system and that of Greenwich. A prime meridian is declared using the -pm parameter, and may be assigned a symbolic name, or the longitude of the alternative prime meridian relative to Greenwich.

Prime meridian declarations are only utilized by the pj_transform() API call, not the pj_inv() and pj_fwd() calls. Consequently the user utility cs2cs does honour prime meridians but the proj user utility ignores them.

The following predeclared prime meridian names are supported. These can be listed using the cs2cs argument -lm:

```
greenwich 0dE
   lisbon 9d07'54.862"W
    paris 2d20'14.025"E
   bogota 74d04'51.3"E
   madrid 3d41'16.48"W
     rome 12d27'8.4"E
     bern 7d26'22.5"E
  jakarta 106d48'27.79"E
    ferro 17d40'W
 brussels 4d22'4.71"E
stockholm 18d3'29.8"E
   athens 23d42'58.815"E
     oslo 10d43'22.5"E
```

Example of use

The location long=0, lat=0 in the Greenwich based lat/long coordinates is translated to lat/long coordinates with Madrid as the prime meridian:

```
cs2cs +proj=latlong +datum=WGS84 \
   +to +proj=latlong +datum=WGS84 +pm=madrid


0 0                               (input)
3d41'16.48"E    0dN 0.000     (output)
```

Datum transformation to WGS84 (towgs84)

Datum shifts can be approximated by 3 parameter spatial translations (in geocentric space), or 7 parameter shifts (translation + rotation + scaling). The parameters to describe this can be described using the towgs84 parameter.

In the three parameter case, the three arguments are the translations to the geocentric location in meters.

For instance, the following demonstrates converting from the Greek GGRS87 datum to WGS84:

```
cs2cs +proj=latlong +ellps=GRS80 +towgs84=-199.87,74.79,246.62 \
   +to +proj=latlong +datum=WGS84


20 35
20d0'5.467"E    35d0'9.575"N 8.570
```

The EPSG database provides this example for transforming from WGS72 to WGS84 using an approximated 7 parameter transformation:

```
cs2cs +proj=latlong +ellps=WGS72 +towgs84=0,0,4.5,0,0,0.554,0.219 \
   +to +proj=latlong +datum=WGS84


4 55
4d0'0.554"E    55d0'0.09"N 3.223
```

The seven parameter case uses delta_x, delta_y, delta_z, Rx - rotation X, Ry - rotation Y, Rz - rotation Z, M_BF - Scaling. The three translation parameters are in meters as in the three parameter case. The rotational parameters are in seconds of arc. The scaling is apparently the scale change in parts per million.

A more complete discussion of the 3 and 7 parameter transformations can be found in the EPSG database (trf_method 9603 and 9606). Within PROJ.4 the following calculations are used to apply the towgs84 transformation (going to WGS84). The x, y and z coordinates are in geocentric coordinates. Three parameter transformation (simple offsets):

```
x[io] = x[io] + defn->datum_params[0];
y[io] = y[io] + defn->datum_params[1];
z[io] = z[io] + defn->datum_params[2];
```

Seven parameter transformation (translation, rotation and scaling):

```
#define Dx_BF (defn->datum_params[0])
#define Dy_BF (defn->datum_params[1])
#define Dz_BF (defn->datum_params[2])
#define Rx_BF (defn->datum_params[3])
#define Ry_BF (defn->datum_params[4])
#define Rz_BF (defn->datum_params[5])
#define M_BF  (defn->datum_params[6])


x_out = M_BF*(x[io] - Rz_BF*y[io] + Ry_BF*z[io]) + Dx_BF;
y_out = M_BF*(Rz_BF*x[io] + y[io] - Rx_BF*z[io]) + Dy_BF;
z_out = M_BF*(-Ry_BF*x[io] + Rx_BF*y[io] +  z[io]) + Dz_BF;
```

Note that EPSG method 9607 (coordinate frame rotation) coefficients can be converted to EPSG method 9606 (position vector 7-parameter) supported by PROJ.4 by reversing the sign of the rotation vectors. The methods are otherwise the same.

Grid Based Datum Adjustments (nadgrids)

In many places (notably North America and Australia) national geodetic organizations provide grid shift files for converting between datums, such as NAD27 to NAD83. These grid shift files include a shift to be applied at each grid location. Actually grid shifts are normally computed based on an interpolation between the containing four grid points.

PROJ.4 currently supports use of grid shift files for shifting between datums and WGS84 under some circumstances. The grid shift table formats are ctable (the binary format produced by the PROJ.4 nad2bin program), NTv1 (the old Canadian format), and NTv2 (.gsb - the new Canadian and Australian format).

Use of grid shifts is specified using the nadgrids keyword in a co-ordinate system definition. For example:

```
cs2cs +proj=latlong +ellps=clrk66 +nadgrids=ntv1_can.dat \
  +to +proj=latlong +ellps=GRS80 +datum=NAD83 << EOF
-111 50
EOF
```

```
  111d0'2.952"W   50d0'0.111"N 0.000
```

In this case the /usr/local/share/proj/ntv1_can.dat grid shift file
was loaded, and used to get a grid shift value for the selected point.

It is possible to list multiple grid shift files, in which case each will
be tried in turn till one is found that contains the point being transformed:

```
cs2cs +proj=latlong +ellps=clrk66 \
      +nadgrids=conus,alaska,hawaii,stgeorge,stlrnc,stpaul \
  +to +proj=latlong +ellps=GRS80 +datum=NAD83 << EOF
-111 44
EOF
```

```
  111d0'2.788"W   43d59'59.725"N 0.000
```

Skipping Missing Grids

The special prefix @ may be prefixed to a grid to make it optional. If
it is not found, the search will continue to the next grid. Normally
any grid not found will cause an error.

For instance, the following would use the ntv2_0.gsb file if available, otherwise it would fallback to using the ntv1_can.dat file:

```
cs2cs +proj=latlong +ellps=clrk66 +nadgrids=@ntv2_0.gsb,ntv1_can.dat \
  +to +proj=latlong +ellps=GRS80 +datum=NAD83 << EOF
-111 50
EOF
```

```
  111d0'3.006"W   50d0'0.103"N 0.000
```

The null Grid

A special null grid shift file is shipped with releases after 4.4.6 (not
inclusive). This file provides a zero shift for the whole world. It
may be listed at the end of a nadgrids file list if you want a zero
shift to be applied to points outside the valid region of all the other

grids. Normally if no grid is found that contains the point to be transformed an error will occur:

```
cs2cs +proj=latlong +ellps=clrk66 +nadgrids=conus,null \
  +to +proj=latlong +ellps=GRS80 +datum=NAD83 << EOF
-111 45
EOF


111d0'3.006"W    50d0'0.103"N 0.000

cs2cs +proj=latlong +ellps=clrk66 +nadgrids=conus,null \
  +to +proj=latlong +ellps=GRS80 +datum=NAD83 << EOF
-111 44
-111 55
EOF


111d0'2.788"W    43d59'59.725"N 0.000
111dW    55dN 0.000
```

Downloading and Installing Grids

The source distribution of PROJ.4 contains only the `ntv1_can.dat` file. To get the set of US grid shift files it is necessary to download an additional distribution of files from the PROJ.4 site, such as proj-nad27–1.1.tar.gz. Overlay it on the PROJ.4 source distribution, and re-configure, compile and install.

The distributed ASCII `.lla` files are converted into binary (platform specific) files that are installed. On Windows using the `nmake /f makefile.vc nadshift` command in the `proj\src` directory to build and install these files.

It appears we can't redistribute the Canadian NTv2 grid shift file freely, though it is better than the NTv1 file. However, end users can download it for free from the NRCan web site.[107]

[107] NTv2 tools and data: `http://loc8.cc/ntv2`

After downloading it, just dump it in the data directory with the other installed data files (usually `/usr/local/share/proj`).

Caveats

Where grids overlap (such as `conus` and `ntv1_can.dat` for instance) the first found for a point will be used regardless of whether it is appropriate or not. So, for instance, `+nadgrids=ntv1_can.dat,conus` would result in the Canadian data being used for some areas in the northern United States even though the `conus` data is the approved data to use for the area. Careful selection of files and file order is necessary. In some cases border spanning datasets may need to be pre-segmented into Canadian and American points so they can be properly grid shifted.

There are additional grids for shifting between NAD83 and various HPGN versions of the NAD83 datum. Use of these haven't been tried recently so you may encounter problems. The `FL.lla`, `WO.lla`, `MD.lla`, `TN.lla` and `WI.lla` are examples of high precision grid shifts. Take care!

Additional detail on the grid shift being applied can be found by setting the `PROJ_DEBUG` environment variable to any value. This will result in output to stderr on what grid is used to shift points, the bounds of the various grids loaded and so forth.

PROJ.4 always assumes that grids contain a shift **to** NAD83 (essentially WGS84). Other types of grids might or might not be usable.

```
cs2cs -f "%.6f" +proj=latlong +datum=NAD83  \
          +to +proj=latlong +datum=NAD83 < input_coord
```

Part IX

Appendix 2 - Data Format
Listings

1

Raster Data Formats

Long Format Name	Code	Create/Georef
Arc/Info ASCII Grid	AAIGRID	Yes/Yes
ACE2	ACE2	No/Yes
ADRG/ARC Digitalized Raster Graphics (.gen/.thf)	ADRG	Yes/Yes
Arc/Info Binary Grid (.adf)	AIG	No/Yes
AIRSAR Polarimetric	AIRSAR	No/No
Magellan BLX Topo (.blx, .xlb)	BLX	Yes/Yes
Bathymetry Attributed Grid (.bag)	BAG	No/Yes
Microsoft Windows Device Independent Bitmap (.bmp)	BMP	Yes/Yes
BSB Nautical Chart Format (.kap)	BSB	No/Yes
VTP Binary Terrain Format (.bt)	BT	Yes/Yes
CEOS (Spot for instance)	CEOS	No/No
DRDC COASP SAR Processor Raster	COASP	No/No
TerraSAR-X Complex SAR Data Product	COSAR	No/No
Convair PolGASP data	CPG	No/Yes
USGS LULC Composite Theme Grid	CTG	No/Yes
Spot DIMAP (metadata.dim)	DIMAP	No/Yes
ELAS DIPEx	DIPEx	No/Yes

DODS / OPeNDAP	DODS	No/Yes
First Generation USGS DOQ (.doq)	DOQ1	No/Yes
New Labelled USGS DOQ (.doq)	DOQ2	No/Yes
Military Elevation Data (.dto, .dt1, .dt2)	DTED	Yes/Yes
Arc/Info Export E00 GRID	E00GRID	No/Yes
ERDAS Compressed Wavelets (.ecw)	ECW	Yes/Yes
ESRI .hdr Labelled	EHdr	Yes/Yes
Erdas Imagine Raw	EIR	No/Yes
NASA ELAS	ELAS	Yes/Yes
ENVI .hdr Labelled Raster	ENVI	Yes/Yes
Epsilon - Wavelet compressed images	EPSILON	Yes/No
ERMapper (.ers)	ERS	Yes/Yes
Envisat Image Product (.n1)	ESAT	No/No
EOSAT FAST Format	FAST	No/Yes
FIT	FIT	Yes/No
FITS (.fits)	FITS	Yes/No
Fuji BAS Scanner Image Fuji	BAS	No/No
Generic Binary (.hdr Labelled)	GENBIN	No/No
Oracle Spatial GeoRaster	GEORASTER	Yes/Yes
GSat File Format	GFF	No/No
Graphics Interchange Format (.gif)	GIF	Yes/No
WMO GRIB1/GRIB2 (.grb)	GRIB	No/Yes
GMT Compatible netCDF	GMT	Yes/Yes
GRASS Rasters	GRASS	No/Yes
GRASS ASCII Grid GRASS	ASCIIGrid	No/Yes
Golden Software ASCII Grid	GSAG	Yes/No
Golden Software Binary Grid	GSBG	Yes/No
Golden Software Surfer 7 Binary Grid	GS7BG	No/No
GSC Geogrid	GSC	Yes/No
TIFF / BigTIFF / GeoTIFF (.tif)	GTiff	Yes/Yes
NOAA .gtx vertical datum shift	GTX	Yes/Yes
GXF - Grid eXchange File	GXF	No/Yes

Hierarchical Data Format Release 4 (HDF4)	HDF4	Yes/Yes
Hierarchical Data Format Release 5 (HDF5)	HDF5	No/Yes
HF2/HFZ heightfield raster	HF2	Yes/Yes
Erdas Imagine (.img)	HFA	Yes/Yes
Image Display and Analysis (WinDisp)	IDA	Yes/Yes
ILWIS Raster Map (.mpr,.mpl)	ILWIS	Yes/Yes
Intergraph Raster	INGR	Yes/Yes
USGS Astrogeology ISIS cube (Version 2)	ISIS2	Yes/Yes
USGS Astrogeology ISIS cube (Version 3)	ISIS3	No/Yes
JAXA PALSAR Product Reader (Level 1.1/1.5)	JAXAPALSAR	No/No
Japanese DEM (.mem)	JDEM	No/Yes
JPEG JFIF (.jpg)	JPEG	Yes/Yes
JPEG-LS	JPEGLS	Yes/No
JPEG2000 (.jp2, .j2k)	JPEG2000	Yes/Yes
JPEG2000 (.jp2, .j2k)	JP2ECW	Yes/Yes
JPEG2000 (.jp2, .j2k)	JP2KAK	Yes/Yes
JPEG2000 (.jp2, .j2k)	JP2MrSID	Yes/Yes
JPEG2000 (.jp2, .j2k)	JP2OpenJPEG	Yes/Yes
JPIP (based on Kakadu)	JPIPKAK	No/Yes
KMLSUPEROVERLAY		Yes/Yes
NOAA Polar Orbiter Level 1b Data Set (AVHRR)	L1B	No/Yes
Erdas 7.x .LAN and .GIS	LAN	No/Yes
FARSITE v.4 LCP Format	LCP	No/Yes
Daylon Leveller Heightfield	Leveller	No/Yes
NADCON .los/.las Datum Grid Shift	LOSLAS	No/Yes
In Memory Raster	MEM	Yes/Yes
Vexcel MFF	MFF	Yes/Yes
Vexcel MFF2	MFF2 (HKV)	Yes/Yes
MG4 Encoded Lidar	MG4Lidar	No/Yes

Multi-resolution Seamless Image Database	MrSID	No/Yes
Meteosat Second Generation	MSG	No/Yes
EUMETSAT Archive native (.nat)	MSGN	No/Yes
NLAPS Data Format	NDF	No/Yes
NITF (.ntf/nsf/gn?/hr?/ja?/jg?, .jn?/lf?/on?/tl?/tp?, etc.)	NITF	Yes/Yes
NetCDF	netCDF	Yes/Yes
NTv2 Datum Grid Shift	NTv2	Yes/Yes
Northwood/VerticalMapper - Classified Grid Format (.grc/.tab)	NWT_GRC	No/Yes
Northwood/VerticalMapper - Numeric Grid Format (.grd/.tab)	NWT_GRD	No/Yes
OGDI Bridge	OGDI	No/Yes
OZI OZF2/OZFX3	OZI	No/Yes
PCI .aux Labelled	PAux	Yes/No
PCI Geomatics Database File	PCIDSK	Yes/Yes
PCRaster	PCRaster	Yes/Yes
Geospatial PDF	PDF	No/Yes
NASA Planetary Data System	PDS	No/Yes
Portable Network Graphics (.png)	PNG	Yes/No
PostGIS Raster (previously WK-TRaster)	PostGISRaster	No/Yes
Netpbm (.ppm,.pgm)	PNM	Yes/No
R Object Data Store	R	Yes/No
Rasdaman	RASDAMAN	No/No
Rasterlite - Rasters in SQLite DB	Rasterlite	Yes/Yes
Swedish Grid RIK (.rik)	RIK	No/Yes
Raster Matrix Format (*.rsw, .mtw)	RMF	Yes/Yes
Raster Product Format/RPF (CADRG, CIB)	RPFTOC	No/Yes
RadarSat2 XML (product.xml)	RS2	No/Yes
Idrisi Raster	RST	Yes/Yes
SAGA GIS Binary format	SAGA	Yes/Yes
SAR CEOS	SAR_CEOS	No/Yes
ArcSDE Raster	SDE	No/Yes
USGS SDTS DEM (*CATD.DDF)	SDTS	No/Yes

SGI Image Format	SGI	Yes/Yes
Snow Data Assimilation System	SNODAS	No/Yes
Standard Raster Product (ASR-P/USRP)	SRP	No/Yes
SRTM HGT Format	SRTMHGT	Yes/Yes
Terragen Heightfield (.ter)	TERRAGEN	Yes/No
EarthWatch/DigitalGlobe .TIL	TIL	No/No
TerraSAR-X Product	TSX	Yes/No
USGS ASCII DEM / CDED (.dem)	USGSDEM	Yes/Yes
GDAL Virtual (.vrt)	VRT	Yes/Yes
OGC Web Coverage Service	WCS	No/Yes
WEBP	WEBP	Yes/No
OGC Web Map Service	WMS	No/Yes
X11 Pixmap (.xpm)	XPM	Yes/No
ASCII Gridded XYZ	XYZ	Yes/Yes

2

Vector Data Formats

Long Format Name	Code	Create/Georef
Aeronav FAA files	AeronavFAA	No/Yes
ESRI ArcObjects	ArcObjects	No/Yes
Arc/Info Binary Coverage	AVCBin	No/Yes
Arc/Info .Eoo (ASCII) Coverage	AVCEoo	No/Yes
Atlas BNA	BNA	Yes/No
AutoCAD DXF	DXF	Yes/No
Comma Separated Value (.csv)	CSV	Yes/No
CouchDB / GeoCouch	CouchDB	Yes/Yes
DODS/OPeNDAP	DODS	No/Yes
EDIGEO	EDIGEO	No/Yes
ESRI Personal GeoDatabase	PGeo	No/Yes
ESRI ArcSDE	SDE	No/Yes
ESRI Shapefile	ESRI Shapefile	Yes/Yes
FMEObjects Gateway	FMEObjects Gateway	No/Yes
GeoJSON	JSON	Yes/Yes
Géoconcept Export	Geoconcept	Yes/Yes
Geomedia .mdb	Geomedia	No/No
GeoRSS	GeoRSS	Yes/Yes
Google Fusion Tables	GFT	Yes/Yes
GML	GML	Yes/Yes

GMT	GMT	Yes/Yes
GPSBabel	GPSBabel	Yes/Yes
GPX	GPX	Yes/Yes
GRASS	GRASS	No/Yes
GPSTrackMaker (.gtm, .gtz)	GPSTrackMake	Yes/Yes
Hydrographic Transfer Format	HTF	No/Yes
Informix DataBlade	IDB	Yes/Yes
INTERLIS	Interlis 1 Interlis 2	Yes/Yes Yes/Yes
INGRES	INGRES	Yes/Yes
KML	KML	Yes/Yes
LIBKML	LIBKML	Yes/Yes
Mapinfo File	MapInfo File	Yes/Yes
Microstation DGN	DGN	Yes/No
Access MDB (PGeo and Geomedia capable)	MDB	No/Yes
Memory	Memory	Yes/Yes
MySQL	MySQL	No/Yes
NAS - ALKIS	NAS	No/Yes
Oracle Spatial	OCI	Yes/Yes
ODBC	ODBC	No/Yes
MS SQL Spatial	MSSQLSpatial	Yes/Yes
OGDI Vectors (VPF, VMAP, DCW)	OGDI	No/Yes
OpenAir	OpenAir	No/Yes
PCI Geomatics Database File	PCIDSK	No/No
PDS	PDS	No/Yes
PostgreSQL SQL dump	PGDump	Yes/Yes
PostgreSQL/PostGIS	PostgreSQL/Pc	Yes/Yes
EPIInfo .REC	REC	No/No
S-57 (ENC)	S57	No/Yes
SDTS	SDTS	No/Yes
Norwegian SOSI Standard	SOSI	No/Yes
SQLite/SpatiaLite	SQLite	Yes/Yes
SUA	SUA	No/Yes
SVG	SVG	No/Yes
UK .NTF UK.	NTF	No/Yes

U.S. Census TIGER/Line	TIGER	No/Yes
VFK data	VFK	No/Yes
VRT - Virtual Datasource	VRT	No/Yes
OGC WFS (Web Feature Service)	WFS	Yes/Yes
X-Plane/Flightgear aeronautical data	XPLANE	No/Yes

Part X

Index

1

Index

Books from Locate Press

The Geospatial Desktop provides a foundational level of knowledge for understanding GIS and the open source desktop mapping applications that are available for use, for free, today.

Learn about vector and raster data, how to convert data, interacting with spatial databases, creating new map data, geoprocessing, scripting, and more.

Special sections include focused learning on the Quantum GIS and GRASS GIS software platforms as well as an introduction to other packages.

The Geospatial Desktop is written by the founder of the Quantum GIS project, so you can rest assured that you will be led by one of the most knowledgeable authors on the subject.

The Quantum GIS Training Manual - Get the jump-start you need to learn this incredibly popular free desktop mapping and GIS toolset.

Comprehensive and structured, your introduction begins with a quick download of example data, making it easy for you to work your way through the concepts and practical exercises, complete with answers and examples.

Ideal for classroom instruction and self-guided learning, included are all the materials needed to run a five day course on Quantum GIS, PostgreSQL and PostGIS.

Content is structured for novice, intermediate and advanced users alike. Seasoned Quantum GIS users will also find tips and new techniques to apply to every mapping project. Windows, Mac OS X, or Linux? It's your choice, this book works for all.

The PyQGIS Programmer's Guide - Extending QGIS just got easier! This book is your fast track to getting started with PyQGIS.

After a brief introduction to Python, you'll learn how to understand the QGIS Application Programmer Interface (API), write scripts, and build a plugin. The book is designed to allow you to work through the examples as you go along. At the end of each chapter you'll find a set of exercises you can do to enhance your learning experience.

The PyQGIS Programmer's Guide is compatible with the version 2.0 API released with QGIS 2.x. All code samples and data are freely available from the book's website. Get started learning PyQGIS today!

Be sure to visit http://locatepress.com for information on new and upcoming titles.

CPSIA information can be obtained
at www.ICGtesting.com
Printed in the USA
BVOW07s0531251116

468704BV00005B/72/P